Crypto Horizons

Beyond Bitcoin: Unraveling the Potential of Altcoins and New Crypto Projects

Maxwell Drake

Table of Contents

INTRODUCTION

Bitcoin is the earliest decentralized digital currency and the embodiment of a revolutionary notion that shook the foundations of existing monetary systems and financial systems in general when it was introduced in 2009. But as the environment surrounding cryptocurrencies continues to change, a new generation of digital assets is developing, each with its own set of characteristics, applications, and potential outcomes. These digital contenders, which are frequently referred to as "altcoins," are more than simply alternatives to Bitcoin; rather, they represent a varied array of innovative projects that are redefining the way we view and interact with value in the digital sphere.

Welcome to "Crypto Horizons: Beyond Bitcoin - Unraveling the Potential of Altcoins and New Crypto Projects." In this book, we go on an adventure that takes us beyond the boundaries of Bitcoin and into the expansive world of alternative cryptocurrencies and new crypto ventures. We investigate the intricacies of their technology, analyze their possible uses, and uncover the difficulties and opportunities that they provide to investors, technologists, and the global financial ecosystem as a whole.

The time has long since past that Bitcoin was the only prominent cryptocurrency in the universe. Alternative cryptocurrencies, such as Ethereum with its smart contract capabilities and privacy-focused coins such as Monero, have emerged on the scene, each bringing with it their own distinct collection of characteristics and use cases. However, the emergence of so many possibilities brings with it an increase in complexity and volatility, as well as the requirement of a deeper level of comprehension. The world of alternative cryptocurrencies can be an exciting but risky one, as it is a place where innovation and speculation collide, and where possibility and risk are intertwined.

In the chapters that are to come, we will provide you with the information that you require in order to successfully traverse this always shifting landscape. We will investigate the many kinds of alternative cryptocurrencies, investigate the underlying technology that enable them, and assess the elements that lead to the success or failure of these cryptocurrencies. The enticing promises of decentralized finance (DeFi) and the complexity of non-fungible tokens (NFTs) are just two examples of the interesting use cases that are being driven by the emergence of cryptocurrencies. In this book, we will explore the exciting use cases that are being driven by these new cryptocurrencies.

However, there are some obstacles in the road ahead. Alternative cryptocurrencies come with their own share of difficulties, just like any other possibility for financial investment. The cryptocurrency industry is notoriously volatile, and the sector for alternative cryptocurrencies is no exception to this rule. The presence of regulatory concerns, scams, and technical vulnerabilities also looms large, necessitating a cautious approach and diligent research prior to diving in.

This book is intended to act as a guide for you, whether you are an experienced crypto enthusiast looking for new horizons or a newbie inquisitive about the possibilities beyond Bitcoin. In this fast-paced and ever-changing industry, we will guide you through investing strategies, risk management, and the tools you need to make informed decisions.

The lines of code that will make up the future of finance are currently being created, and they will be run on decentralized networks. As we explore the potential of altcoins and developing cryptocurrencies, we would like to ask you to join us in our pursuit of the unknown, our embrace of the opportunities, and our discovery of the hidden gems that have the ability to change the future financial landscape.

Therefore, let's get started on this journey together, as we go beyond the shadow of Bitcoin and into the bustling world of alternative cryptocurrencies and emerging crypto projects.

CHAPTER I

Understanding Altcoins and Emerging Cryptocurrencies

Definition of altcoins and their differentiation from Bitcoin

In the fast-evolving world of digital currencies, Bitcoin has long held the mantle as the pioneer, the trailblazer that ignited the spark of global cryptocurrency adoption. Yet, as the technology underpinning blockchain networks matures, many digital assets have emerged in the wake of Bitcoin's success, collectively known as "altcoins" or alternative coins. Altcoins, a portmanteau of "alternative" and "coins," represent a spectrum of cryptocurrencies that extend beyond Bitcoin, not just in name but also in their intricate technological structures, distinct purposes, and varied functionalities.

At its most fundamental, an altcoin is defined simply as any cryptocurrency other than Bitcoin. Yet, this apparent simplicity belies the complex and multifaceted nature of the altcoin landscape. These digital entities can be categorized into diverse groups based on their unique features, blockchain protocols, and intended applications, resulting in a diverse tapestry of innovation that extends far beyond Bitcoin's origins.

Perhaps one of the most pivotal distinctions between altcoins and Bitcoin lies in their foundational technology and the architecture of their respective blockchains. Bitcoin, conceived by the mysterious Satoshi Nakamoto, introduced the world to the concept of a decentralized and tamper-proof ledger through its innovative proof-of-work consensus mechanism. Altcoins, however, have not been content to replicate this approach simply. Instead, they have ventured into uncharted territory, experimenting with various consensus mechanisms such as proof-of-stake, delegated proof-of-stake, and proof-of-authority. Ethereum, the second-largest cryptocurrency by market capitalization, catalyzed a seismic shift in the cryptocurrency space by introducing the notion of "smart contracts." This groundbreaking feature enabled developers to build decentralized applications (dApps) atop its blockchain, ushering in a new era where blockchain capabilities transcended simple transactions.

Moreover, the surge of altcoins has frequently been fueled by a desire to address perceived limitations present within Bitcoin. While Bitcoin's primary identity rests as a store of value and medium of exchange, altcoins have explored a spectrum of purposes. Privacy-centric altcoins like Monero and Zcash have incorporated advanced cryptographic techniques to augment transaction privacy and anonymity, filling a void in Bitcoin's transparency. Other altcoins have homed in on scalability, striving to process more transactions per second to overcome the scalability concerns occasionally plaguing Bitcoin.

Another crucial dimension in which altcoins diverge from Bitcoin pertains to the type of blockchain they operate on. A subset of altcoins runs on dedicated, independent blockchains, each distinguished by its own set of protocols and rules that differentiate it from Bitcoin and other altcoins. Litecoin, for example, emerged as a response to Bitcoin, offering faster block confirmation times as an inherent feature. Conversely, Ripple utilizes a consensus mechanism that deviates from the traditional mining process, introducing a fresh approach to achieving network consensus.

However, it's imperative to recognize that not all altcoins function on their standalone blockchains. A significant segment of altcoins exists in the form of tokens built atop established blockchains. Ethereum's introduction of the ERC-20 token standard was mainly instrumental in this development. These tokens inherit their parent blockchain's infrastructure, allowing for various functionalities. The subsequent wave of Initial Coin Offerings (ICOs) brought tokens into the limelight, providing projects with a novel means of fundraising and creating tokens with specific utilities within decentralized ecosystems.

Despite the proliferation of altcoins and the promising ventures they embody, debates have persisted within the cryptocurrency community about their value and purpose. Critics contend that numerous altcoins lack intrinsic utility, created primarily to ride the wave of cryptocurrency enthusiasm rather than offering substantive solutions. While it's undeniable that not all altcoins will weather the storms of time and market dynamics, some have carved out niches that demonstrate genuine innovation. These niches span a broad spectrum, encompassing decentralized finance (DeFi), non-fungible tokens (NFTs), supply chain management, identity verification, and many other applications.

In the grand tapestry of the cryptocurrency ecosystem, altcoins emerge as the multifaceted offspring of Bitcoin's pioneering success. Each altcoin has a distinctive genetic code characterized by its technological innovations, nuanced purposes, and unique features. While these digital assets have their origins in Bitcoin's groundbreaking blueprint, they transcend its boundaries, exploring new avenues and redefining the limits of blockchain technology.

In conclusion, altcoins embody blockchain's evolution, representing a diverse array of digital assets that transcend the boundaries set by Bitcoin. Their diversity is underscored by the various consensus mechanisms, blockchain architectures, and intended use cases that distinguish them. The journey beyond Bitcoin leads us through a landscape of innovation, where these alternative coins continually redefine privacy, scalability, functionality, and purpose. The ongoing evolution of the altcoin realm paints a vivid picture of the dynamic nature of the cryptocurrency ecosystem, a realm where innovation thrives and new possibilities await exploration.

Historical context: The evolution of altcoins and their purpose

The emergence of altcoins marks a pivotal chapter in the narrative of the cryptocurrency revolution, a history that has transcended the boundaries of traditional finance, challenging conventions, and giving rise to new paradigms. As we look deeper into the historical context of altcoins, we discover a story of creativity, aspiration, and the relentless goal of pushing beyond the boundaries of what can be accomplished with digital currency.

The story begins with the birth of Bitcoin, the groundbreaking creation of the enigmatic Satoshi Nakamoto in 2009. As the first cryptocurrency to leverage blockchain technology, Bitcoin ushered in a new era of peer-to-peer transactions, characterized by decentralization, immutability, and transparency. Yet, even in its infancy, Bitcoin was not without its limitations. The scalability debate, the need for increased transaction speed, and concerns about energy consumption cast a shadow over the seemingly limitless potential of Nakamoto's brainchild.

It was within this context that altcoins entered the scene. The first altcoin, Namecoin, made its appearance in 2011. Designed to leverage blockchain technology for domain name registration, Namecoin sought to decentralize a service previously reliant on centralized entities. While its impact remained relatively modest, Namecoin set a precedent by demonstrating that the underlying technology behind Bitcoin could be repurposed for endeavors beyond mere transactions.

As the years unfolded, the landscape saw the rise of Litecoin, often touted as the "silver to Bitcoin's gold." Created by Charlie Lee in 2011, Litecoin distinguished itself by its faster block generation time and adoption of the "scrypt" algorithm, which diverged from Bitcoin's "SHA-256." This marked the first instance of altcoins differentiating themselves through ideological variations and tangible technological distinctions that addressed Bitcoin's limitations. Litecoin became a proving ground for the experimentation and innovation that would drive the evolution of altcoins.

The years 2013 and 2014 saw an explosion of altcoins; a period often referred to as the "altcoin boom." Peercoin introduced the concept of proof-of-stake consensus, aiming to address Bitcoin's energy-intensive proof-of-work mechanism. Ripple emerged as a digital payment protocol to enable fast and cost-effective cross-border transactions. Dogecoin, a playful coin inspired by a popular internet meme, garnered a dedicated community and utilized its unique branding for charitable initiatives.

The sheer diversity of altcoins during this era underscored the growing realization that blockchain technology could be harnessed for various applications, ranging from serious financial instruments to lighthearted endeavors that captured the internet's imagination. While many altcoins came and went, this period laid the groundwork for the diverse ecosystem of digital assets that would emerge in subsequent years.

The evolution of altcoins gained renewed momentum with the advent of Ethereum in 2015. Ethereum's introduction of smart contracts revolutionized the potential applications of blockchain technology. Now, altcoins weren't just about creating variations on Bitcoin's core features; they were about developing platforms that could support decentralized applications, automated agreements, and more. Ethereum's initial coin offering (ICO) raised substantial funds, galvanizing interest in altcoins to finance innovative projects.

The subsequent years witnessed an explosion in the altcoin space, with projects like Monero emphasizing privacy, EOS focusing on scalability, and Cardano prioritizing academic rigor in its development. Additionally, the DeFi (decentralized finance) movement, which gained significant traction in the late 2010s, further underscored the versatile potential of altcoins. DeFi platforms like Compound, MakerDAO, and Uniswap exemplified how altcoins could disrupt traditional financial systems, offering lending, borrowing, and trading functionalities.

The proliferation of altcoins, however, had its challenges. The altcoin landscape became a breeding ground for scams and pump-and-dump schemes fueled by speculation and a lack of regulatory oversight. The term "shitcoin" emerged to denote altcoins with questionable utility and credibility, highlighting the need for discernment within this rapidly evolving ecosystem.

In recent years, the concept of altcoins has matured. The term "altcoin" has shifted from denoting mere alternatives to Bitcoin to representing an array of digital assets with distinct purposes and technological innovations. Altcoins are no longer just experimental projects but engines of innovation driving blockchain technology's evolution. Ethereum's ongoing transition to Ethereum 2.0, designed to improve scalability and sustainability, is a testament to the dynamic and continuous development of the altcoin realm.

In conclusion, the historical context of altcoins is a tale of transformation, ingenuity, and purpose. These alternative coins emerged as a response to the perceived limitations of Bitcoin, exploring diverse applications, from privacy and scalability to decentralized finance and beyond. The altcoin landscape continues to evolve, shaped by technological breakthroughs, market trends, and regulatory developments. Altcoins are no longer mere imitations; they are catalysts for change, challenging the norms of traditional finance and pushing the boundaries of what is possible in the digital age. As the altcoin journey unfolds, we can only speculate on the innovations and disruptions that lie ahead, but one thing remains clear: the story of altcoins is far from reaching its final chapter.

Categories of altcoins: Forks, tokens, and independent blockchains

The world of cryptocurrencies is a vast and dynamic ecosystem, home to an array of digital assets that extend beyond the confines of Bitcoin. These alternative cryptocurrencies, or "altcoins," are not just diverse digital tokens; they encompass a spectrum of innovative projects, each with its distinct purpose, technology, and potential. Within the realm of altcoins, a classification emerges that categorizes them into three primary groups: forks, tokens, and independent blockchains. This classification not only showcases the versatility of altcoins but also highlights the various ways in which they interact with and diverge from the original Bitcoin blueprint.

One of the most noteworthy categories of altcoins is forks. Forks occur when a new blockchain version is created by changing the original code. This may take place for a variety of causes, ranging from technical upgrades to ideological disagreements within the community. Two primary types of forks emerge: hard forks and soft forks.

A hard fork results in a permanent divergence in the blockchain, creating two distinct chains. Bitcoin Cash, which emerged from a hard fork of Bitcoin in 2017, aimed to address scalability concerns by increasing the block size. This decision led to a new blockchain with separate rules, distinct from Bitcoin's. Similarly, Bitcoin SV (Satoshi Vision) emerged due to disagreements within the Bitcoin Cash community, leading to a further divergence in the blockchain's development trajectory.

In contrast, a soft fork involves backward-compatible blockchain protocol changes. This means that nodes running the new software can still communicate with nodes using the older software. Litecoin's Segregated Witness (SegWit) upgrade is an example of a soft fork. SegWit aimed to improve Bitcoin's scalability by altering the transaction structure, allowing more transactions to fit within a single block.

Another significant category within the altcoin landscape is tokens. Unlike forks that operate on their blockchains, tokens are created on existing blockchain platforms. Ethereum's introduction of the ERC-20 token standard marked a pivotal moment in the development of tokens. This standard established a set of rules and functionalities that tokens must adhere to, allowing for seamless integration with Ethereum's ecosystem.

Initial Coin Offerings (ICOs), a method of raising funds when projects offer their tokens to investors in return for money to finance development, are frequently linked to tokens. These tokens may symbolize a range of assets, from security tokens that signify ownership in a business or asset to utility tokens that allow access to platform services. Notable tokens include Binance Coin (BNB), which was initially created to facilitate trading on the Binance exchange, and Chainlink (LINK), which focuses on providing decentralized data oracle services.

Tokens also play a pivotal role in the burgeoning decentralized finance (DeFi) movement. Platforms like Compound and Aave offer lending, borrowing, and liquidity provision services through tokens incentivizing users to participate in the ecosystem. These tokens provide access to services and enable holders to participate in governance decisions, shaping the platform's future.

The third category of altcoins comprises those that operate on their independent blockchains. Unlike tokens and forks, which leverage existing blockchain platforms, these altcoins forge their paths by developing new blockchain networks with unique features and protocols.

Litecoin stands as one of the earliest examples of an independent blockchain altcoin. Created by Charlie Lee in 2011, Litecoin aimed to address some of the limitations of Bitcoin, such as transaction speed. Through its Scrypt proof-of-work algorithm and faster block confirmation times, Litecoin offered a distinct alternative for those seeking a quicker and lighter cryptocurrency.

While often sparking debates about its classification as a cryptocurrency, Ripple operates as an independent blockchain altcoin. Focused on facilitating fast and cost-effective cross-border transactions, Ripple's blockchain does not rely on traditional mining but employs a unique consensus mechanism to validate transactions. This divergence from the Bitcoin model highlights how altcoins can deviate fundamentally while still sharing the overarching concept of blockchain technology.

In the grand tapestry of altcoins, the categories of forks, tokens, and independent blockchains are testaments to the versatility and innovation that characterize the cryptocurrency space. While they all stem from the foundation laid by Bitcoin, these altcoins branch out into distinct trajectories, addressing challenges, experimenting with new functionalities, and reshaping the digital landscape. The existence of these diverse categories underscores the dynamic nature of the cryptocurrency evolution, where innovation knows no bounds and the possibilities continue to expand with each passing day.

As the altcoin ecosystem evolves, it's essential to recognize that these categories are not static. Projects continually push boundaries, introducing hybrid models that bridge the gaps between forks, tokens, and independent blockchains. As the boundaries between these categories blur, the cryptocurrency landscape gains even greater depth and complexity, promising a future where altcoins continue to evolve, innovate, and redefine the realms of possibility.

The role of altcoins in the broader crypto ecosystem

In digital currencies, Bitcoin has long been hailed as the trailblazer, the harbinger of a decentralized financial future. Yet, as the cryptocurrency landscape matures, a constellation of alternative digital assets, appropriately named "altcoins," has emerged, reshaping the contours of the broader crypto ecosystem. These altcoins are not mere imitations of Bitcoin; they are unique entities, each with a distinct role and purpose that collectively contribute to the evolving narrative of decentralized finance.

Altcoins bring diversity to the cryptocurrency universe, opening doors to many applications that extend beyond the foundational use case of Bitcoin as a digital currency. This diversification serves as a response to the limitations perceived in Bitcoin, whether it's scalability, privacy, or programmability. For instance, altcoins like Litecoin and Bitcoin Cash focus on faster transaction speeds and lower fees, addressing one of Bitcoin's longstanding challenges. Monero and Zcash take a privacy-centric approach, using advanced cryptographic techniques to enhance transaction anonymity, an area where Bitcoin falls short due to its public ledger.

Moreover, altcoins allow for specialization in specific sectors. For example, Ethereum's smart contract capabilities enable the creation of decentralized applications (dApps) and facilitate the issuance of new tokens through Initial Coin Offerings (ICOs). This specialization empowers developers to build applications that cater to various industries, from decentralized finance (DeFi) platforms that offer lending and borrowing services to non-fungible token (NFT) marketplaces that revolutionize digital ownership.

Altcoins serve as hotbeds of innovation and experimentation. While Bitcoin laid the foundation for blockchain technology, altcoins take this foundation and build upon it, exploring novel consensus mechanisms, governance structures, and cryptographic features. Through experimentation, altcoins pave the way for new ideas and technologies that may return to the broader crypto ecosystem, benefiting the entire industry.

For instance, projects like Cardano emphasize rigorous academic research and peer-reviewed development, fostering a culture of scientific rigor in blockchain technology. This commitment to research and innovation has the potential to enhance the credibility of the broader crypto ecosystem, driving it closer to mainstream adoption.

Altcoins are at the forefront of expanding the use cases of cryptocurrencies. While Bitcoin's primary identity is often as a store of value and a medium of exchange, altcoins extend the spectrum of utility. For example, DeFi platforms built on Ethereum offer a range of financial services like decentralized lending, yield farming, and liquidity provision. These platforms enable users to engage with financial instruments and services in a trustless and permissionless manner, reshaping the financial landscape.

NFTs, another revolutionary concept brought to life by altcoins, disrupt digital ownership and provenance. Altcoins like Flow and Solana have facilitated the creation of NFT marketplaces that enable artists, gamers, and creators to tokenize and sell digital assets, from digital art to virtual real estate. This innovative use case showcases the transformative power of altcoins in unlocking value from previously untapped avenues.

The presence of altcoins fosters healthy competition within the cryptocurrency ecosystem. This competition encourages projects to improve, innovate, and deliver real-world value continually. Just as startups in the tech industry challenge and inspire one another to evolve, altcoins keep each other on their toes, driving advancements in technology, usability, and features.

Furthermore, altcoins provide a sandbox for blockchain developers and entrepreneurs to experiment with new ideas. This experimentation leads to technological advancements and exposes vulnerabilities and weaknesses that must be addressed. The collective evolution driven by altcoins benefits the entire crypto space, including Bitcoin, by spurring innovation and enhancing the overall robustness of the ecosystem.

The role of altcoins in the broader crypto ecosystem is that of a collaborative and transformative force. They extend the boundaries of what is possible in the digital realm, offering specialized solutions, fostering innovation, expanding use cases, and igniting healthy competition. Altcoins stand as a testament to the flexibility of blockchain technology, demonstrating that it's not just a single invention but a canvas upon which a myriad of possibilities can be painted.

As the altcoin landscape evolves, it's important to remember that these digital assets are interconnected threads in the larger fabric of the crypto ecosystem. Just as diverse ecosystems in nature thrive due to the interconnectedness of their components, the crypto landscape flourishes through the symbiotic relationship between Bitcoin and altcoins. Together, they form a dynamic tapestry that reflects the collective aspirations of a global community pushing the boundaries of finance, technology, and human ingenuity.

CHAPTER II

Evaluating the Potential of Altcoins

Factors influencing the value and potential of altcoins

Altcoins have emerged in the dynamic world of cryptocurrencies, wherein innovation and disruption go hand in hand, as a testament to the evolutionary potential of the digital financial landscape. These alternative cryptocurrencies, often referred to as altcoins, come in diverse forms, each striving to carve its niche within the broader crypto ecosystem. However, the value and potential of altcoins are not merely determined by chance; instead, they are influenced by a myriad of interconnected factors that shape their trajectory, adoption, and impact on the global financial system.

At the heart of any altcoin's value proposition lies its technological innovation. Innovations can range from novel consensus mechanisms that address the energy consumption concerns of proof-of-work systems, to advanced cryptographic techniques that enhance privacy and security, and to smart contract platforms that open doors to decentralized applications. For instance, Ethereum's introduction of smart contracts transformed the blockchain landscape by enabling programmable agreements and decentralized applications that extend beyond simple transactions.

The potential for technological innovation does not solely rest on the creators of altcoins; it also hinges on the vibrancy of the development community and their ability to adapt and iterate. The speed at which a project can implement upgrades, resolve vulnerabilities, and respond to emerging challenges often correlates with its perceived value and potential.

The value of an altcoin is intricately linked to its utility and real-world applications. Altcoins that offer solutions to existing problems or introduce new possibilities stand a better chance of gaining traction and driving adoption. For instance, altcoins that cater to decentralized finance (DeFi) have gained substantial attention by providing platforms for lending, borrowing, and trading, bypassing traditional financial intermediaries.

Likewise, altcoins focusing on specific industries, such as supply chain management, identity verification, or the Internet of Things (IoT), can potentially disrupt and revolutionize those sectors. The value proposition of these altcoins rests on their ability to solve practical problems and create efficiencies, ultimately driving demand for their use.

Market demand and user adoption play a crucial role in determining the value and potential of altcoins. As cryptocurrencies become more mainstream, their adoption as a means of payment, store of value, or investment vehicle can significantly impact their valuation. Bitcoin's ascent from being a niche experiment to a globally recognized digital asset underscores the power of user adoption in influencing the value of altcoins.

Factors that drive user adoption include ease of use, security, and creating ecosystems that support and incentivize users to participate. Altcoins that forge partnerships with traditional financial institutions, payment processors, and merchants can foster user confidence and drive widespread adoption.

The regulatory landscape is another critical factor that shapes the value and potential of altcoins. Regulatory clarity and compliance with local laws can impact the legality of altcoin usage, exchanges, and investment.

Altcoins that navigate regulatory challenges effectively and work within established frameworks have a better chance of thriving and gaining acceptance in the broader financial ecosystem.

However, regulatory uncertainty can also present challenges. Altcoins that face strict regulations or bans in certain jurisdictions may encounter obstacles in achieving widespread adoption and value appreciation. The evolving nature of cryptocurrency regulations adds a layer of complexity that altcoin projects must navigate.

In the volatile world of cryptocurrencies, market sentiment and investor perception are pivotal in determining altcoin value. Positive news, technological breakthroughs, and successful partnerships can generate enthusiasm and drive prices higher. Conversely, negative events, security breaches, or regulatory crackdowns can lead to sharp declines in value.

Investor perception is intertwined with team credibility, transparency, and the project's overall vision. Altcoins that effectively communicate their purpose, demonstrate a strong development community, and remain transparent in their operations tend to inspire confidence and garner a positive perception.

For altcoins aiming for broad adoption, scalability—the capacity of a blockchain to manage growing transaction volumes—is essential. As demand for transactions and usage grows, the ability of an altcoin's network to maintain speed and low fees becomes paramount. Projects prioritizing scalability through innovative consensus mechanisms or layer-2 solutions position themselves for long-term value appreciation.

Additionally, network effects contribute to the value and potential of altcoins. A thriving and engaged user base and a robust ecosystem of applications and services can create a self-reinforcing cycle where increased usage leads to higher demand, driving further adoption and value.

The value and potential of altcoins are not determined by a single factor, but by a complex interplay of technological innovation, real-world applications, market demand, regulatory environment, investor sentiment, scalability, and network effects. These factors intertwine to shape the trajectory of altcoins, from their inception to their impact on the broader crypto ecosystem. As the cryptocurrency landscape continues to evolve, understanding these factors becomes paramount for investors, developers, and enthusiasts seeking to navigate the dynamic world of altcoins.

Technology and innovation: Exploring unique features of different altcoins

In the ever-evolving landscape of cryptocurrencies, innovation is the driving force that propels the industry forward. Altcoins, the diverse array of digital assets beyond Bitcoin, exemplify this spirit of innovation by introducing unique features and technologies that extend the boundaries of what blockchain technology can achieve. From advanced privacy mechanisms to novel consensus algorithms, each altcoin brings its distinct flavor to the table, offering solutions to challenges and unlocking new possibilities within the broader crypto ecosystem.

Privacy has been a central concern within the cryptocurrency space since its inception. While Bitcoin transactions are pseudonymous, they are not truly private, as anyone can trace the flow of funds on the public ledger. In response, privacy-focused altcoins have emerged, each employing advanced cryptographic techniques to enhance transaction anonymity.

Monero, for instance, utilizes ring signatures and confidential transactions to obfuscate transaction details, rendering them virtually untraceable. This heightened privacy comes at the cost of larger transaction sizes and increased computational requirements. Similar to this, Zcash uses zero-knowledge proofs to enable users to demonstrate the legitimacy of a transaction without disclosing any private data. These privacy features resonate with users seeking financial autonomy and confidentiality in their transactions.

Scalability-focused cryptocurrencies were developed as a response to Bitcoin's scalability issues, which were manifested as slow speed of transactions and high fees during times of network congestion. These altcoins implement novel consensus mechanisms and network structures to increase transaction throughput and minimize bottlenecks.

EOS, for example, employs a delegated proof-of-stake (DPoS) consensus mechanism where selected block producers validate transactions. This approach enhances scalability by reducing the time required for consensus. Similarly, Solana introduces a unique consensus mechanism known as Proof of History (PoH), which creates a chronological record of events outside the blockchain. This feature assists in reducing network latency and increasing the efficiency of transaction processing.

The development of smart contract platforms, which allow for the building of decentralized apps (dApps), is perhaps one of the most groundbreaking contributions of altcoins. Ethereum's innovation with smart contracts opened the door to a new paradigm where blockchain technology becomes a foundation for programmable agreements and self-executing contracts.

Altcoins like Cardano and Polkadot further this vision by emphasizing interoperability and scalability. Cardano, for instance, employs a layered architecture and aims to implement a peer-reviewed development process, drawing from academic research to enhance its capabilities. On the other hand, Polkadot introduces a multi-chain infrastructure that allows different blockchains to interoperate, facilitating the seamless exchange of assets and data.

Altcoins have also pioneered the concept of tokenization, enabling the representation of real-world assets on the blockchain. These tokens can encompass a range of assets, from traditional financial instruments to unique digital items.

Tezos, for example, facilitates tokenized assets through its smart contracts, enabling the creation of security tokens that represent ownership in real-world assets like real estate or company equity. Similarly, Flow focuses on tokenizing digital assets, allowing creators and artists to tokenize and sell their digital content as non-fungible tokens (NFTs). This opens up avenues for the monetization of digital creations and the establishment of verifiable ownership rights.

Stablecoins represent another category of altcoins that stabilize the volatile cryptocurrency market. These tokens are typically pegged to traditional assets like fiat currencies or commodities, offering a reliable unit of value while retaining the benefits of blockchain technology.

Tether (USDT) and USD Coin (USDC) are prominent examples of stablecoins that mirror the value of the US dollar. However, innovations within this space extend beyond simple pegs. MakerDAO's DAI, for instance, maintains stability through an algorithmic system of collateralization and debt issuance, creating a decentralized stablecoin without direct reliance on fiat reserves.

The altcoin landscape is a testament to the power of technological innovation. Each altcoin weaves a unique thread into the intricate tapestry of the broader crypto ecosystem. Whether it's enhancing privacy, improving scalability, enabling smart contracts, tokenizing assets, or providing stability, altcoins introduce a diverse array of features that address the challenges and aspirations of this evolving industry.

As the altcoin space continues to evolve, it showcases the malleability of blockchain technology, capable of being shaped into various forms to suit specific use cases. These altcoins collectively propel the cryptocurrency ecosystem forward, pushing the boundaries of innovation, adoption, and utility. As investors, developers, and enthusiasts navigate this complex landscape, they witness the boundless potential that emerges when technology meets imagination.

Market demand and real-world applications

In the grand tapestry of the cryptocurrency landscape, altcoins stand as the vibrant threads that weave innovation, utility, and possibility into the broader fabric of decentralized finance. As Bitcoin's pioneering success paved the way for the proliferation of digital assets, altcoins emerged as distinctive entities, each with its purpose and potential. Central to their value proposition is the interplay between market demand and real-world applications—a dynamic relationship that drives adoption, shapes use cases, and reshapes traditional financial paradigms.

Market demand serves as the heartbeat of the altcoin ecosystem, influencing their value, liquidity, and overall trajectory. Just as traditional financial markets are guided by supply and demand dynamics, the cryptocurrency market thrives on the collective sentiment and appetite of investors, traders, and enthusiasts.

The demand for altcoins is multifaceted. Speculative investors seek to capitalize on price volatility, aiming for short-term gains driven by price fluctuations. This speculative demand can lead to significant price swings, creating opportunities for traders and contributing to market volatility. However, the broader, sustainable demand stems from the value these altcoins bring to the table through their real-world applications.

The value proposition of altcoins extends far beyond speculative trading, resonating with real-world applications that disrupt and transform traditional industries. One of the most prominent examples of real-world applications is the decentralized finance (DeFi) movement. DeFi platforms built on altcoins like Ethereum offer various financial services, from lending and borrowing to decentralized exchanges and yield farming. These platforms provide users a new level of financial autonomy, allowing them to access services without relying on intermediaries.

In cross-border transactions, altcoins offer practical solutions to the inefficiencies of traditional remittance systems. Ripple's XRP, for instance, has positioned itself as a bridge currency for facilitating fast and cost-effective international transfers. Its ability to settle transactions within seconds challenges the conventional cross-border payment methods that often take days.

Tokenization is another area where altcoins demonstrate their real-world impact. Projects like Chainlink enable the integration of real-world data into blockchain applications, a vital aspect for industries like supply chain management and insurance. By bridging the gap between blockchain and physical assets, tokenization enhances transparency, efficiency, and traceability.

Altcoins cater to niche markets and specialized use cases that were previously underserved by traditional financial systems. Privacy-focused altcoins like Monero and Zcash address the demand for confidential transactions, ensuring user privacy in an increasingly digital world. These altcoins resonate with individuals who prioritize financial confidentiality and anonymity.

Furthermore, altcoins have carved their niches in the gaming and entertainment sectors. For example, Enjin Coin (ENJ) provides a platform for creating and trading blockchain-based virtual assets, enabling the ownership of in-game items with real-world value. This intersection of gaming and blockchain illustrates how altcoins tap into existing industries and reshape their dynamics.

Regulatory environments and geographical considerations also influence market demand for altcoins.

Cryptocurrency adoption is unique globally, with different regions embracing or restricting digital assets to varying degrees. Altcoins that offer solutions that align with specific regulatory frameworks are more likely to gain traction in those jurisdictions.

In countries with volatile economies and unstable local currencies, altcoins can serve as an alternative store of value and medium of exchange. Venezuelans turning to cryptocurrencies like Dash and Bitcoin to hedge against hyperinflation exemplify this trend. Similarly, altcoins can provide financial inclusion to unbanked populations in regions lacking traditional financial infrastructure.

The relationship between market demand and real-world applications of altcoins is symbiotic—a harmonious interplay where value is derived from the tangible benefits these digital assets offer. Altcoins are not merely speculative vehicles; they represent a paradigm shift in finance, unlocking opportunities that traditional systems cannot provide. As altcoins find their niches, innovate in various sectors, and address practical challenges, they inspire market demand that propels their adoption.

This dynamic dance between market demand and real-world applications underscores the maturation of the cryptocurrency ecosystem. Altcoins are not isolated experiments; they are agents of change, altering the course of industries, democratizing finance, and ushering in a new era of decentralized possibilities. The symbiotic relationship between market demand and real-world utility creates a virtuous cycle where adoption drives value, and value drives adoption—an ongoing narrative that reshapes the way we perceive and interact with the world of finance.

Team and development community: Assessing the credibility and expertise

In the intricate tapestry of the cryptocurrency landscape, where innovation and disruption are the guiding principles, the role of the development team and community behind altcoins takes center stage. Beyond the technological features and use cases, the credibility and expertise of the individuals driving altcoin projects profoundly influence their success, adoption, and long-term potential. A robust and capable team can transform an ambitious concept into a tangible reality while a thriving community ensures ongoing development, resilience, and adaptability. As investors and enthusiasts navigate the vast altcoin ecosystem, understanding the importance of evaluating the team and development community becomes paramount.

The development team is the backbone of any altcoin project. Their collective expertise, vision, and dedication shape the project's technical foundations, security protocols, and roadmap. The team's composition, experience, and ability to execute the project's objectives are critical factors that influence the project's credibility and potential.

Transparency is key when assessing the team's credibility. A trustworthy team provides clear and verifiable information about their identities, backgrounds, and past projects. This transparency fosters trust among investors and the broader community, minimizing the risk of potential scams or fraudulent activities.

A diverse team with expertise spanning various domains, including blockchain technology, cryptography, economics, and legal compliance, can lend legitimacy to the project. A well-rounded team is better equipped to navigate the challenges of altcoin development and respond effectively to the evolving needs of the crypto ecosystem.

The development team's track record is pivotal in evaluating its capabilities. Previous successful projects, contributions to open-source software, and innovations in the blockchain space demonstrate the team's competence and commitment to the field. Past accomplishments indicate the team's ability to overcome challenges and deliver on their promises.

Execution is a critical aspect of team evaluation. A capable team sets clear milestones, communicates progress transparently, and delivers updates consistently. Timely execution showcases the team's commitment to its vision and engenders confidence among investors and users.

The development community surrounding an altcoin project is a testament to its vitality and potential for growth. A thriving community extends beyond the development team, encompassing enthusiasts, contributors, supporters, and users actively engaging with the project.

Community engagement fosters collaboration, innovation, and collective problem-solving. The more active and engaged the community, the more likely the project will receive valuable feedback, identify potential issues, and iterate on its features. A strong community acts as a support system that amplifies the project's impact and can contribute to marketing and advocacy efforts.

The degree of decentralization within the community is a noteworthy factor to consider. A project that encourages community-driven development and governance empowers a broader range of stakeholders to participate in decision-making processes. This not only enhances the project's democratic nature but also reduces the risk of centralization, which could undermine the project's long-term sustainability.

Community initiatives, such as hackathons, bounties, and grants, also indicate a commitment to nurturing talent and fostering innovation. These initiatives attract developers, researchers, and entrepreneurs who contribute to the project's growth while expanding the pool of expertise.

Open and transparent communication between the development team and the community is essential. Regular updates, progress reports, and roadmaps give stakeholders insights into the project's development trajectory. Transparency builds trust and helps investors make informed decisions based on the project's current status and future plans.

Transparency also extends to the project's funding model. Clear information about how the project is funded and how resources are allocated ensures accountability and mitigates concerns about financial mismanagement.

The team and development community are the heartbeat of altcoin projects, dictating their trajectory, credibility, and potential. Evaluating the development team's expertise, assessing their track record, and understanding their commitment to execution are critical steps for investors seeking projects with long-term viability.

Equally significant is assessing the community's engagement, diversity, and decentralization. A strong and vibrant community contributes to the project's development and acts as a bulwark against challenges and setbacks.

As the altcoin landscape continues to evolve, the importance of the team and development community remains constant. Beyond the buzz of technological features and market trends, these individuals' dedication, innovation, and collaboration shape the narrative of each altcoin, influencing its impact on the broader cryptocurrency ecosystem and the world of finance at large.

CHAPTER III

The Challenges and Risks of Altcoin Investments

Volatility and market risks associated with altcoins

In the ever-evolving world of cryptocurrencies, altcoins have emerged as dynamic and innovative digital assets that extend beyond the foundational Bitcoin. While altcoins promise to reshape industries, democratize finance, and introduce groundbreaking technologies, they also come with unique challenges and risks. Among these challenges, one of the most notable is the inherent volatility and market risks synonymous with the altcoin landscape. As investors, enthusiasts, and participants navigate this realm, understanding the nature of volatility and the associated market risks is crucial for making informed decisions and managing expectations.

The volatility of the cryptocurrency market is well known, and altcoins are no different. Unlike traditional financial markets, where price fluctuations are typically more measured, the cryptocurrency arena is characterized by rapid and often extreme price swings. This volatility arises from a combination of factors, including speculative trading, relatively small market capitalizations, and the developing nature of the industry.

While volatility can offer opportunities for significant gains, it also poses substantial risks. Altcoin prices can soar to astronomical heights within a short period, only to experience sharp corrections that wipe out gains just as quickly. This volatility can lead to emotional trading, where investors make impulsive decisions based on short-term price movements rather than sound fundamentals.

Several factors contribute to the volatility and market risks associated with altcoins. One of the primary drivers is market sentiment. Positive news, such as partnerships, technological breakthroughs, or adoption by major players, can send prices soaring. Conversely, negative news, security breaches, regulatory crackdowns, or market manipulation can trigger steep declines.

Liquidity, or the ease of buying or selling an asset without causing significant price changes, also impacts volatility. Altcoins with lower liquidity are more susceptible to sharp price swings, as larger trades can disproportionately affect the market.

Moreover, the interconnected nature of the cryptocurrency market amplifies the influence of Bitcoin's price movements on altcoins. Often referred to as the "Bitcoin Dominance Effect," altcoins tend to follow suit when Bitcoin experiences extreme price fluctuations.

Regulatory developments play a significant role in driving altcoin volatility. The lack of clear regulations and differing regulatory stances across jurisdictions can lead to uncertainty and market instability. For instance, announcements of potential bans or restrictions on altcoin trading in certain countries can trigger panic selling and extreme price volatility.

Regulatory measures can also impact the functioning of altcoin projects. Regulatory compliance costs, legal challenges, and the need to adapt to changing regulations can divert resources away from development and hinder project progress.

The fundamentals of an altcoin project also influence its volatility. Projects with solid use cases, innovative technologies, and active development teams tend to fare better during market downturns. Conversely, altcoins with vague or unrealistic goals, lack of transparency, or weak development teams are more likely to suffer from price declines and loss of investor confidence.

Skepticism within the broader market can also contribute to altcoin volatility. Investors may question the viability of specific projects, leading to rapid sell-offs and market panic. Altcoins with ambitious claims but little to no substance often fall victim to heightened skepticism and ultimately lose value.

Market manipulation is a persistent concern within the cryptocurrency space. Many altcoins' relatively low market capitalizations make them susceptible to price manipulation by a few large holders, commonly called "whales." These individuals or entities can execute large trades that create artificial price movements, inducing panic buying or selling among other investors.

In some cases, coordinated efforts within online communities, particularly on social media platforms, can also amplify price volatility. Pumps and dumps, where a group of investors artificially inflates the price of an altcoin before selling off their holdings, are examples of market manipulation tactics that contribute to volatility.

Given the inherent volatility and market risks associated with altcoins, managing risks becomes a paramount consideration for investors and participants. Diversification, or spreading investments across different assets, can help mitigate losses from extreme price swings. Thorough research, understanding project fundamentals, and evaluating the development team's credibility are essential for making informed investment decisions.

Setting clear investment goals and risk tolerance is crucial. Investors should avoid acting impulsively and instead concentrate on the long-term potential of projects rather than making quick judgments based on short-term price fluctuations.

Moreover, staying informed about market trends, regulatory developments, and technological advancements can provide a clearer understanding of the factors driving volatility and risk.

The altcoin landscape is a realm of opportunity, innovation, and transformation but also a space rife with volatility and market risks. While the potential for substantial gains is undeniable, the flip side is the risk of significant losses. Investors must approach the altcoin market with caution, diligence, and a willingness to learn.

Understanding the factors driving volatility—market sentiment, liquidity, regulatory developments, project fundamentals, and market manipulation—is critical to making informed decisions. By acknowledging the risks and taking proactive measures to manage them, investors can navigate the altcoin realm more adeptly, harnessing the potential for growth while minimizing the impact of market turbulence.

Regulatory challenges and legal considerations

With its promise of financial innovation and decentralization, the world of cryptocurrencies has captivated the imagination of individuals and institutions alike. Altcoins, the diverse array of digital assets beyond Bitcoin, have emerged as pioneers of change, introducing novel technologies and disrupting traditional financial systems. However, this innovative landscape is not exempt from the intricate regulatory challenges and legal considerations governing the broader financial ecosystem. As altcoins strive to find their place within the global economy, they must navigate a complex regulatory environment that spans jurisdictions, addresses security concerns, and balances innovation with consumer protection.

The regulatory landscape for altcoins is far from uniform, with different countries and regions adopting a range of approaches to their treatment. Some nations have embraced altcoins with open arms, recognizing their potential for economic growth and technological advancement. Others remain cautious, concerned about the potential risks associated with these novel digital assets.

This lack of uniformity poses challenges for altcoin projects and investors alike. Altcoins that thrive in one jurisdiction may face regulatory hurdles or bans in another, leading to uncertainty and potential disruption of business models. As a result, altcoin projects often find themselves at the intersection of legal compliance and technological innovation.

One of the primary challenges for altcoins is determining their legal classification, mainly whether they are considered securities. Securities regulations are designed to protect investors by imposing disclosure requirements and registration procedures on investment opportunities. The classification of an altcoin as a security has far-reaching implications, subjecting the project to extensive legal requirements and regulatory oversight.

The Howey Test, a widely used framework established by the U.S. Supreme Court, is often employed to determine whether an altcoin qualifies as a security. This test determines if a financial commitment contains the expectation of profits from the hard work of others. Altcoins that meet these criteria may be subject to securities regulations, impacting their token issuance, trading, and overall operations.

AML and KYC standards, which are intended to prevent illicit activity like money laundering and terrorism financing, are also applicable to altcoins. Exchanges and platforms that facilitate the trading of altcoins are often required to implement robust AML and KYC procedures, including verifying the identities of their users and reporting suspicious transactions.

This presents challenges for altcoin projects that prioritize privacy and anonymity. Privacy-focused altcoins like Monero and Zcash, which utilize advanced cryptographic techniques to obscure transaction details, may face difficulties complying with AML and KYC regulations. Striking a balance between user privacy and regulatory compliance remains an ongoing challenge.

Consumer protection is a significant concern within the altcoin ecosystem. As altcoin projects launch initial coin offerings (ICOs) or token sales, investors are exposed to potential risks, including fraudulent schemes and scams. Regulatory authorities worldwide have taken steps to mitigate these risks by issuing guidelines and advisories, educating the public, and taking legal action against fraudulent projects.

Altcoin projects must prioritize transparency and provide accurate information to investors. Clear communication about project goals, use cases, team backgrounds, and risks associated with investment can help build trust and ensure that investors make informed decisions.

The borderless nature of cryptocurrencies introduces unique challenges related to jurisdictional conflicts and cross-border transactions. Altcoins are accessible to users worldwide, bypassing traditional financial intermediaries. However, this global reach also exposes them to diverse regulatory regimes, each with its interpretation of how altcoins should be treated.

Cross-border transactions involving altcoins raise questions about taxation, jurisdiction, and international cooperation in regulating these digital assets. The lack of standardized regulations and international agreements can lead to legal uncertainties and compliance challenges for altcoin projects and users.

While regulatory challenges can pose obstacles to altcoin projects, some jurisdictions have embraced innovative approaches to foster technological advancement and consumer protection. Regulatory sandboxes, for example, provide a controlled environment where startups and fintech firms can test their products and services under relaxed regulations. These sandboxes allow altcoin projects to innovate and demonstrate their viability while collaborating with regulators to address potential risks.

Countries that foster innovation through sandboxes or similar initiatives provide altcoin projects with an opportunity to iterate on their technologies and business models while engaging with regulatory authorities to ensure compliance.

The regulatory challenges and legal considerations surrounding altcoins underscore the delicate balance between innovation and accountability. Altcoins represent the convergence of technology and finance, and as such, they must navigate a complex web of regulations that differ from one jurisdiction to another. This balance requires collaboration between altcoin projects, regulatory authorities, and legal experts.

As the altcoin landscape evolves, altcoin projects must prioritize legal compliance, transparency, and consumer protection. This approach safeguards investors and ensures that altcoins can realize their potential as drivers of financial innovation. Regulatory challenges may be formidable, but with the right strategies, collaboration, and adherence to best practices, altcoin projects can navigate the regulatory maze and contribute to transforming the global financial ecosystem.

Scams and fraudulent projects: How to identify and avoid them

The allure of altcoins, with their promise of innovation, financial empowerment, and technological breakthroughs, has captured the attention of investors and enthusiasts worldwide. However, this dynamic landscape is not immune to a darker side—scams and fraudulent projects that prey on unsuspecting participants. As the altcoin ecosystem evolves, so do the tactics of malicious actors seeking to exploit the enthusiasm surrounding these digital assets. Understanding the red flags and adopting vigilant practices is essential for safeguarding investments, protecting personal information, and contributing to the integrity of the broader altcoin space.

The spectrum of altcoin-related scams is wide-ranging, from simple Ponzi schemes to elaborate projects with sophisticated marketing tactics. Scammers often exploit the lack of regulatory oversight and the excitement surrounding new projects to create an illusion of legitimacy. Recognizing the diversity of scams is the first step in staying informed and vigilant.

Ponzi schemes, a classic form of fraud, promise unreasonably high returns on investment, often luring participants with the allure of quick riches. These scams rely on the investments of new participants to pay returns to earlier investors, creating a cycle of dependency that inevitably collapses when new investments dry up. Investors should be cautious of projects that promise guaranteed profits with minimal risk. Unrealistic return claims, especially those that seem too good to be true, often indicate fraudulent schemes that exploit the greed and impatience of unsuspecting individuals.

Initial coin offerings (ICOs) and token sales, legitimate fundraising methods for altcoin projects, have also been exploited by scammers. Fraudulent schemes may create fake websites, whitepapers, and social media profiles, mimicking fair altcoin projects to deceive investors into sending funds. Researching the authenticity of ICOs is essential. Scrutinize the project's team, check for discrepancies in official communication channels, and verify the project's presence on reputable platforms. A lack of clear information, absence of verifiable team members, and an overly aggressive marketing approach are red flags that should not be ignored.

Impersonation scams involve malicious actors pretending to be influential figures in the altcoin community, often using fake social media profiles or emails. They may promise investment opportunities, exclusive deals, or insider information in exchange for funds or personal information. Always verify the identity of individuals before engaging in any financial transactions. Confirm the legitimacy of social media accounts, cross-reference contact details with official project communication channels, and be cautious when sharing personal information online.

Pump and dump schemes involve artificially inflating the price of an altcoin through coordinated efforts within online communities, only to sell off holdings at the peak of the price surge. These schemes manipulate market sentiment and create a false sense of urgency, leading investors to make impulsive decisions. Recognizing sudden, unsustainable price spikes and overly enthusiastic endorsements within online communities can help investors identify potential pump and dump schemes. Engaging in thorough research and avoiding hasty decisions based on market hype is crucial.

Educating oneself about the common tactics scammers use is pivotal in avoiding fraudulent projects. Consider the following strategies to identify and steer clear of altcoin-related scams:

Thorough Research: Research the project's team, backgrounds, technological claims, and use cases. Legitimate projects are transparent about their goals and technological features.

Verifiable Identities: Verify team members' identities through official social media accounts, professional profiles, and online presence. The lack of verifiable team information is a red flag.

Official Communication Channels: Use official communication channels, such as the project's website or verified social media accounts, to gather information and updates. Be cautious of information received through private messages or unofficial channels.

Community Engagement: Engage with the project's community and online forums to gauge its credibility and legitimacy. Scrutinize endorsements and recommendations.

Realistic Claims: Be wary of altcoin projects that promise guaranteed high returns, particularly within short timeframes. Unrealistic claims are often indicative of fraudulent schemes.

Security Measures: Ensure that the altcoin project and related platforms have robust security measures in place, including secure websites, encryption, and two-factor authentication.

Cautious Investment: Invest only what you can afford to lose. Avoid investing based on FOMO (Fear of Missing Out) or market hype.

Independent Research: Rely on multiple sources of information, independent reviews, and third-party analysis to validate claims made by the altcoin project.

Regulatory Compliance: Verify that the project adheres to relevant regulations and guidelines. Projects that disregard regulatory compliance may pose higher risks.

Altcoins represent a realm of innovation and possibility but also require a cautious and informed approach. The world of digital assets is marred by scams and fraudulent projects seeking to exploit the unwary. By recognizing the red flags, staying vigilant, and adopting a discerning mindset, investors and enthusiasts can protect their investments, contribute to the integrity of the altcoin ecosystem, and ensure that the journey within this transformative landscape remains one of discovery, growth, and responsible engagement.

Lack of liquidity and exchange listing challenges

The altcoin landscape, an arena of dynamic digital assets poised to reshape industries and redefine financial paradigms, presents both innovation and obstacles. Amid the potential for groundbreaking advancements, altcoin projects grapple with a significant hurdle—the lack of liquidity and the intricacies of securing listings on cryptocurrency exchanges. While altcoins promise to revolutionize traditional financial systems, they often find their path obstructed by liquidity constraints and the demanding process of gaining exposure on reputable trading platforms. Delving into the ramifications of these challenges is crucial for altcoin projects seeking visibility and for investors navigating the dynamic universe of digital assets.

Liquidity, a cornerstone of any thriving financial market, catalyzes efficient price discovery, seamless trading execution, and the ability to swiftly convert assets into cash without causing excessive price fluctuations. Within the context of altcoins, liquidity denotes the presence of readily available buy and sell orders at various price levels, facilitating frictionless transactions for traders and investors alike. Yet, the liquidity landscape in the altcoin market is far from uniform. Established projects like Bitcoin and Ethereum enjoy ample liquidity, while smaller and newer altcoins often grapple with inadequate trading volumes, leading to difficulties for traders seeking to enter or exit positions without incurring significant price slippage.

Numerous factors contribute to the challenges in achieving liquidity within altcoin markets. The most apparent among them is the sheer diversity of the altcoin space. With many projects competing for attention, trading volumes are dispersed across many assets, resulting in shallow markets for many altcoins.

Additionally, altcoins that cater to niche use cases or target specific industries may struggle to amass a substantial user base and trading activity. This lack of adoption and awareness further compounds the liquidity dilemma, entrapping altcoins in a cycle where insufficient liquidity discourages potential traders and investors from participating.

Gaining visibility on cryptocurrency exchanges is a pivotal gateway for altcoin projects to overcome liquidity challenges. These exchanges operate as intermediaries that facilitate the buying and selling of digital assets, providing a platform for traders and investors to access altcoins. However, the journey to securing a listing on prominent exchanges is fraught with obstacles. For altcoin projects, attaining a listing on a major exchange can confer legitimacy, amplify visibility, and augment liquidity. Nevertheless, exchanges meticulously uphold strict listing criteria to ensure the quality and authenticity of the assets they support. These criteria often encompass factors such as the project's technological innovation, market demand, community engagement, and adherence to regulatory standards.

The path toward securing a listing on reputable exchanges is fraught with challenges for altcoin projects. One significant barrier is the intensely competitive nature of the process. With many altcoins vying for limited exchange slots, capturing the attention of exchanges becomes a formidable undertaking. Well-established projects and those boasting robust community support might enjoy an advantage in this race, leaving emerging and lesser-known altcoins at a disadvantage.

Moreover, exchanges commonly impose listing fees, ranging from a few thousand to several million dollars, contingent upon the exchange's reputation and global reach. These fees can pose a substantial financial burden for smaller altcoin projects, further compounding the liquidity challenge. While the prospect of exchange listings is enticing, the financial barriers can deter potentially promising projects from accessing the broader market.

Regulatory considerations also exert a substantial influence on the exchange listing process. As exchanges strive to mitigate legal risks, they increasingly emphasize regulatory compliance. Altcoin projects that lack a robust framework for adhering to regulatory requirements or fail to meet these stipulations may encounter challenges in securing listings. In this context, exchanges prioritize minimizing potential legal liabilities over supporting assets that might not align with prevailing regulations.

To surmount the liquidity deficit and navigate the labyrinthine path to exchange listings, altcoin projects can consider adopting several strategies. Building robust fundamentals, including advanced technology, clear use cases, and a vibrant community, can bolster a project's appeal to exchanges. Active engagement with the community generates interest and demand, capturing the attention of exchanges. Additionally, some altcoin projects establish liquidity pools, where participants provide liquidity in return for rewards, thereby enhancing trading activity and incentivizing exchanges to list the asset. Diversifying the exchange strategy by targeting both major and smaller reputable exchanges can offer initial exposure and liquidity. Prioritizing regulatory compliance and transparency enhances credibility and augments the prospects of securing exchange listings.

In conclusion, the lack of liquidity and the challenges associated with securing exchange listings shed a light on the altcoin landscape's intricacies. Although these challenges pose formidable hurdles, they do not render altcoin projects inert. Projects that invest in establishing strong fundamentals, cultivating community engagement, and navigating the regulatory landscape are better poised to surmount liquidity constraints and secure listings on reputable exchanges.

A keen awareness of liquidity limitations and potential risks linked to lesser-known projects is imperative for investors. Verifying that an altcoin project is listed on reputable exchanges and possesses an active community provides a degree of assurance concerning its legitimacy and potential for growth.

Ultimately, the journey for altcoins to overcome liquidity challenges and secure exchange listings underscores the transformative potential of technology and innovation. As the altcoin ecosystem continues to evolve, the pursuit of liquidity and visibility remains a driving force behind the endeavor to reshape financial systems, democratize asset accessibility, and usher in a new era of decentralized possibilities.

CHAPTER IV

Investing Strategies for Altcoins

Fundamental analysis: Researching altcoins based on technology, team, and use cases

Alternative cryptocurrencies, or altcoins, have arisen as a dynamic force of innovation within the expansive world of cryptocurrencies. They present a diverse assortment of digital assets outside the prominent presence of Bitcoin. Investors and enthusiasts alike are confronted with a key task as the cryptocurrency landscape continues to expand, and that burden is undertaking a comprehensive fundamental analysis in order to make informed judgments among the myriad of projects that are accessible. An altcoin's fundamental analysis requires a deep dive into the complexities of its underlying technology, as well as the experience and knowledge of its development team and the applicability of its use cases. This thorough investigation makes it possible for stakeholders to traverse the complex cryptocurrency ecosystem and differentiate between projects that have the potential to succeed and those that are more likely to fail. Those who are interested in engaging with alternative cryptocurrencies in a responsible and strategic manner are well advised to familiarize themselves with the relevance of fundamental analysis.

The underlying technology of an altcoin is the most important aspect of that cryptocurrency because it determines its functioning, level of security, and scalability potential. An altcoin's technological base, including aspects such as its consensus mechanism, blockchain architecture, and smart contract capabilities, must be thoroughly investigated as part of a fundamental analysis. This requires taking a technological deep dive.

One of the most important aspects to take into account is the consensus mechanism, which is the system that ensures transactions are valid and adds them to the blockchain. There are many different consensus mechanisms, some of which include Proof of Work, Proof of Stake, and Delegated Proof of Stake. These processes all offer varied degrees of decentralization, energy efficiency, and security. It is absolutely necessary to do an analysis to determine whether or not the chosen consensus mechanism is appropriate for the project's objectives.

Additionally, it is essential to have a solid grasp of the blockchain architecture of the alternative cryptocurrency. The ability of an alternative cryptocurrency to process a high volume of transactions is a critical factor in its scalability, speed, and transaction costs. A forward-thinking attitude is demonstrated through projects that provide novel solutions to scalability issues in blockchains, such as layer 2 solutions or sharding.

The development team of an alternative cryptocurrency is the engine that powers the cryptocurrency's technological progress and its operational success. The fundamental analysis include investigating the team's level of experience and skill, as well as their track record and level of dedication to the project's vision.

The level of technical expertise possessed by the team is of the utmost significance. It is more likely that a challenge can be navigated and the development of an alternative cryptocurrency can be driven by a team that is transparent and whose members possess relevant industry knowledge as well as a history of successful projects. A well-rounded decision can be achieved through the collaborative efforts of a broad team that includes developers, researchers, and business professionals.

The level of dedication and involvement that the team has should also be taken into consideration by investors. Teams that are responsive and involved, as well as those that keep an active line of communication open with their community, indicate a dedication to the expansion and success of the project.

Evaluating the use cases and possible market demand for an alternative cryptocurrency is an important component of fundamental analysis. To have a lasting influence, alternative cryptocurrencies need to find solutions to problems or inefficiencies that exist in the real world.

Projects with concrete use cases that address previously identified problems or improve existing procedures have a better chance of being adopted. Investigating whether or if the alternative cryptocurrency provides a solution that is not already available, improves upon previously developed technology, or disrupts industries is one way to gain insight into its potential for success.

In addition, it is essential to have a solid awareness of the audience for the altcoin as well as the demand for the solutions it offers. A competitive edge can be gained by projects that cater to underserved segments while also aligning themselves with the current market trends. It is possible to further bolster the altcoin's legitimacy by doing research into partnerships and collaborations that validate the altcoin's utility.

Legal difficulties and regulatory compliance are of the utmost importance when it comes to alternative cryptocurrencies. The fundamental analysis should include an assessment to see if the alternative coin is in compliance with the applicable rules, so that any potential legal difficulties can be avoided.

It is crucial to have a solid understanding of the altcoin's approach to regulatory compliance, particularly with regard to AML (Anti-Money Laundering) and KYC (Know Your Customer) policies. Alternative cryptocurrencies that place a high priority on compliance and transparency exhibit a dedication to functioning within the bounds of the law.

The potential risks that are related with the alternative cryptocurrency should also be analyzed by investors. These dangers can take the form of technology vulnerabilities, competition from other projects, unstable markets, and difficulties in scaling up operations. Stakeholders are able to manage their investment portfolios more efficiently and make educated decisions when they have a thorough awareness of the risks that they face.

The application of fundamental analysis is essential to responsible and purposeful interaction with alternative cryptocurrencies. Investors and cryptocurrency enthusiasts may confidently traverse the complex altcoin ecosystem if they study the technology, development team, use cases, market demand, regulatory compliance, as well as risks associated with a particular alternative cryptocurrency.

While fundamental analysis can provide helpful insights, it is essential to recognize that investing in alternative cryptocurrencies comes with its own set of inherent risks.

The intricacy of the technology and the dynamics of the market, in conjunction with the volatility of the cryptocurrency market, highlights the significance of conducting thorough research and exercising due diligence at all times.

In conclusion, the world of alternative cryptocurrencies is a domain of both opportunity and risk. Individuals are provided with the resources necessary to differentiate between opportunities that hold promise and those that pose a threat, which contributes to the continuous evolution of cryptocurrencies as a force of transformational innovation in the global financial environment.

Technical analysis: Reading price charts and identifying entry/exit points

Altcoins have arisen as an attractive route for traders and investors seeking opportunities beyond the sphere of Bitcoin in the ever-evolving environment of cryptocurrency investment. This is because altcoins have developed as an alternative cryptocurrency to Bitcoin. The practice of analyzing price charts, patterns, and indicators in order to arrive at well-informed choices is known as technical analysis. As the altcoin market continues to gain traction, market participants will find that technical analysis is a crucial tool in their armory.

Mastering the art of technical analysis has the promise of discovering ideal entry and exit points, analyzing market patterns, and managing risks for individuals who are navigating the complexities of altcoin investing. This can be accomplished by minimizing the likelihood of losses. To participate in the cryptocurrency alternative market in a responsible and strategic manner, it is essential to have a solid understanding of the key principles and procedures of technical analysis.

A key principle of technical analysis is the conviction that examination of past price data along with trade volume can yield valuable insights about the direction in which prices are likely to move in the future. This strategy is founded on the assumption that pricing patterns and trends are reflective of market psychology, investor sentiment, and the supply and demand dynamics at play in an economy.

Price charts are used as the canvas for technical analysts to paint their forecasts on. The line chart and the candlestick chart are the two forms of price charts that are used the most frequently. In the field of technical analysis, candlestick charts are particularly popular due to their capacity to express a great deal of information within the confines of a single candle. These charts illustrate the opening, closing, highest, as well as lowest prices for each candlestick over the course of a specified time frame, which reveals important insights into the sentiment of the market.

Price patterns, which are recurrent forms that foreshadow prospective price movements, are scrutinized in great detail by technical analysts. Patterns may be bullish, which indicates that prices are trending higher, bearish, which indicates that prices are trending downward, or neutral. The head and shoulders, double tops and bottoms, and also triangles are three of the most common and well-known patterns.

For example, a "head and shoulders" pattern, which is a formation with three peaks that resembles the head and shoulders of a human figure, typically indicates a shift from an upward trend to a downward trend. This can happen when there is a change in the direction of the trend. Recognizing and accurately understanding these patterns can help investors make more informed investment decisions and better predict prospective price movements.

Indicators are mathematical computations that are produced from previous price and volume data. They offer insights into the momentum of the market, the strength of the trend, and the possibility of reversals. These indications are helpful for gaining a better understanding of the underlying causes that are driving price changes as well as pinpointing the best entry and exit points.

The Relative Strength Index, commonly referred to as RSI, is a well-known momentum indicator that can be utilized to determine whether or not an alternative cryptocurrency has been overbought or oversold. If the value of the RSI goes beyond a specific barrier, this may be an indication that the alternative coin has been overbought and is due for a price correction. On the other hand, a low RSI score could indicate that an oversold position exists, which could be interpreted as a buying opportunity.

Moving averages help identify trends as well as potential reversals by averaging price data over a predetermined period of time and smoothing it out. A "golden cross," for instance, is formed when a short-term moving average passes over a long-term moving average, which indicates a possible upward trend.

Support and resistance levels, in technical analysis, are essential components because they indicate areas of the market where price movements may be met with opposition or experience reversals. Support levels are price settings at which demand has traditionally been sufficiently robust to prevent further price decreases from occurring. Resistance levels are places in the market at which supply tends to exceed demand, putting a stop to further price increases.

Recognizing these levels can help investors make judgments based on more accurate information. For example, if the price of a cryptocurrency is getting close to a level that has historically acted as resistance, there may be a push to sell it, which may cause the price to turn around. On the other hand, a bounce off of a support level can indicate that there is an opportunity to buy.

When it comes to determining the best times to buy and sell alternative cryptocurrencies, technical analysis is an invaluable tool. When prices are stable for an extended length of time or when certain patterns begin to appear, which may signal a change in trend, investors frequently look to enter positions. When indications point to the possibility of overbought situations or when the price is getting close to historical resistance levels, their goal may be to get out of their positions.

The process of determining entry and exit points in an altcoin trade needs a balanced grasp of the technical background of the cryptocurrency, the sentiment of the larger market, and one's level of risk tolerance. When making judgments, it can be helpful to make use of a number of different price patterns, indicators, and support and resistance levels all at the same time.

For investors and traders of alternative cryptocurrencies who are attempting to traverse the complex world of cryptocurrency markets, technical analysis is an extremely useful tool. Market players can improve their capacity to make well-informed judgments on entry and exit points by understanding price charts, detecting trends, and applying indicators. This will allow them to better control their level of risk.

It is of the utmost importance to understand that technical analysis is not devoid of its inherent limitations. Even the most experienced technical analysts may find it difficult to make accurate predictions in the cryptocurrency market due to its high degree of volatility and frequent price swings. In addition, technical analysis is purely focused on historical price data, to the exclusion of any consideration of external factors such as legislative shifts, macroeconomic events, or technology breakthroughs, all of which have the ability to affect the values of alternative cryptocurrencies.

In conclusion, technical analysis is an asset that should be included in the toolset of anyone who deals with alternative cryptocurrencies. Traders and investors can equip themselves with the tools necessary to approach the altcoin market with a well-rounded perspective by combining technical analysis with fundamental research, risk management tactics, and a discernment-based attitude. Mastering the fundamentals of technical analysis provides a foundation for responsible and purposeful engagement in the cryptocurrency arena. This is especially important given the environment, which is marked by innovation, volatility, and the possibility for transformation.

Diversification: Building a balanced altcoin portfolio

In cryptocurrency investing, where innovation and volatility intersect, the allure of altcoins beckons both seasoned traders and newcomers. Altcoins, or alternative cryptocurrencies to Bitcoin, represent a spectrum of digital assets that offer diverse use cases, technological innovations, and investment opportunities. As investors navigate this complex landscape, the concept of diversification emerges as a guiding principle that advocates for spreading investments across multiple altcoins to mitigate risks and maximize potential returns. Careful attention must be given to factors including risk tolerance, investment objectives, market trends, and the specifics of each project while constructing a balanced altcoin portfolio. Understanding the significance of diversification is pivotal for those seeking to navigate the altcoin market with prudence and strategic foresight.

In order to spread investments among a variety of assets and lessen the impact of losses from any one investment, diversification is an important investment principle. In the context of altcoins, diversification extends to allocating investments across a range of projects, each with its unique features, strengths, and potential for growth. This strategy aids in reducing the risks brought on by volatility in the market, project-specific setbacks, or changes in industry trends.

Diversification seeks to strike a balance between the pursuit of potential gains and the management of potential losses. While no strategy can entirely eliminate risks, diversification offers a means of navigating the altcoin market's inherent unpredictability with a level-headed approach.

One of the primary considerations when building a diversified altcoin portfolio is an individual's risk tolerance and investment goals. Risk tolerance refers to an investor's ability to withstand fluctuations in the market without making hasty decisions driven by fear or panic. If you have a higher risk appetite, you might allocate a huge percentage of your portfolio to riskier, high-potential altcoins, but if you have a lower risk appetite, you might concentrate on safer, more established projects.

Investment goals vary from individual to individual. Some seek short-term gains through active trading, while others aim for long-term growth and accumulation. The balance between risk and reward shifts according to these goals. Those pursuing short-term gains might allocate a portion of their portfolio to altcoins with high trading volume and potential for rapid price fluctuations. Long-term investors, on the other hand, might emphasize altcoins with robust fundamentals and the potential for sustainable growth over time.

Diversification within the altcoin market extends to understanding the various categories of projects. In addition to decentralized finance (DeFi), supply chain management, non-fungible tokens (NFTs), gaming, and other applications, altcoins have a wide range of use cases. Each category presents its own set of opportunities and challenges.

A variety of projects from several categories may be present in a portfolio that has been properly diversified. This approach not only spreads risk but also positions the investor to capitalize on the potential of diverse sectors within the blockchain and cryptocurrency ecosystem. For example, a portfolio might include DeFi tokens, NFT-focused altcoins, and projects targeting scalability solutions.

The foundation of effective diversification lies in meticulous research and analysis. Each altcoin within a portfolio should undergo fundamental analysis to evaluate its technological innovation, use case, development team, market demand, and regulatory compliance.

Understanding each project's intrinsic value and growth potential informs the allocation of investments.

Furthermore, monitoring market trends and staying informed about shifts in industry sentiment can influence diversification decisions. Technological advancements, regulatory changes, and macroeconomic events influence cryptocurrency markets. Remaining attuned to these dynamics enables investors to make timely portfolio adjustments.

Balancing the allocation of investments within a diversified altcoin portfolio requires a thoughtful approach. While no one-size-fits-all formula exists, several strategies can guide the allocation process.

One common strategy is the "core-satellite" approach. This involves allocating most of the portfolio to core holdings—established, reputable altcoins with strong fundamentals and long-term growth potential. The remaining portion is allocated to satellite holdings—smaller positions in higher-risk, higher-reward altcoins. This approach balances stability with the potential for substantial gains.

Another approach is the "equal-weighting" strategy, where each altcoin in the portfolio receives an equal allocation. This strategy can be suitable for those who want to spread risk evenly across their investments without making judgments about individual projects' potential.

Diversification is not a one-time endeavor; it requires ongoing monitoring and adaptation. The altcoin market is dynamic, with projects evolving, market trends shifting, and new opportunities emerging. Regularly reviewing the performance and prospects of each altcoin in the portfolio is essential.

Adjustments to the portfolio's allocation may be necessary as the market landscape changes. This might involve reallocating funds from underperforming assets to those showing more significant promise. Staying informed and maintaining a flexible approach allows investors to make decisions that align with their investment goals and the evolving altcoin market.

In the realm of altcoin investing, diversification is a guiding principle that fosters a balanced and strategic approach. Investors can reduce risks, take advantage of a variety of opportunities, and align their portfolios with their risk tolerance and investing goals by distributing their investments among a variety of cryptocurrencies.

It is vital to emphasize that diversification only partially eliminates risks. Cryptocurrency markets remain subject to volatility, regulatory developments, and technological advancements that can impact prices. Responsible diversification is not about entirely eliminating risks but optimizing risk-reward profiles and preparing for a range of potential outcomes.

Diversification offers a framework for responsible and informed engagement in a landscape where market fluctuations match innovation and transformative potential. The altcoin ecosystem is a canvas of possibility, and building a balanced altcoin portfolio equips investors with the tools to navigate this realm with prudence, foresight, and a measured approach to risk-taking.

Long-term vs. short-term strategies: Pros and cons

In the vibrant landscape of cryptocurrency investing, altcoins have emerged as a dynamic avenue, offering diverse opportunities beyond the behemoth presence of Bitcoin. As investors engage with this evolving ecosystem, a crucial decision looms—choosing between long-term and short-term strategies for altcoin investment. These strategies represent distinct approaches to capitalizing on the potential of altcoins, each with advantages and challenges. Long-term investing involves holding altcoins for extended periods, while short-term trading entails more frequent buying and selling to exploit price fluctuations. Understanding the pros and cons of these strategies is essential for investors seeking to navigate the altcoin market with strategic clarity and financial wisdom.

Long-term investing, often referred to as "HODLing" (a play on the word "hold"), revolves around purchasing altcoins with the intent of holding onto them for an extended period, often measured in years. This strategy is underpinned by the belief that well-chosen altcoins' intrinsic value and growth potential will result in significant gains over time.

One of the primary advantages of a long-term approach is the potential for substantial returns. Altcoins with robust fundamentals, innovative technology, and practical use cases can appreciate in value as adoption and demand increase. By holding through market fluctuations and short-term volatility, long-term investors position themselves to capitalize on the long-term growth trajectory of promising projects.

Moreover, long-term investing requires less active involvement than short-term trading. This approach is well-suited for individuals who do not have the time, expertise, or inclination for frequent market monitoring and trading execution. It also aligns with a patient mindset, as investors focus on the potential for value to accumulate over time rather than on immediate gains.

While long-term investing offers potential benefits, it has its drawbacks. One of the most significant challenges is the uncertainty surrounding altcoins' long-term success. The cryptocurrency landscape is characterized by rapid technological advancements, regulatory developments, and market dynamics that can impact the viability of projects. Holding onto altcoins that fail to meet their intended goals can result in significant losses.

Furthermore, long-term investors may experience emotional challenges during periods of market volatility. Altcoin prices can exhibit dramatic fluctuations, and watching the value of investments decrease can test an investor's resolve. Emotional reactions can lead to impulsive decisions, such as panic selling during downturns or making hasty decisions based on fear or greed.

Short-term trading, also referred to as day trading or swing trading, involves more frequent buying and selling of altcoins to capitalize on short-term price movements. Traders aim to exploit price volatility, entering and exiting positions within hours, days, or weeks. This strategy is driven by technical analysis, patterns, and indicators that help traders anticipate price trends.

One of the primary advantages of short-term trading is the potential for quick and frequent gains. Altcoin prices can experience substantial fluctuations over short periods, presenting opportunities to profit from upward and downward movements. Traders who read price charts and patterns effectively can execute well-timed trades to maximize returns.

Short-term trading also allows for active decision-making and rapid adjustments to market developments. Traders can respond swiftly to breaking news, market sentiment shifts, and other catalysts that impact altcoin prices. This agility enables traders to capitalize on opportunities as they arise.

While short-term trading can be lucrative, it has its challenges. One of the most significant drawbacks is the risk of making incorrect predictions. The altcoin market is unpredictable, and even the most sophisticated technical analysis cannot guarantee accurate forecasts. Traders who make wrong calls can experience substantial losses.

Additionally, short-term trading requires a high level of skill, market knowledge, and discipline. Traders must monitor markets consistently, analyze price charts, and execute trades precisely. The fast-paced nature of short-term trading can lead to stress, burnout, and emotional decision-making if not managed effectively.

The decision between a long-term and short-term strategy hinge on an individual's risk tolerance, investment goals, time commitment, and expertise. Long-term investing aligns well with patient investors seeking potential long-term growth, while short-term trading appeals to those who thrive in a fast-paced, active trading environment.

Investors who opt for long-term strategies should prioritize thorough fundamental analysis, evaluating altcoins' technology, use cases, development teams, and market demand. They should also develop a strong mindset to weather market fluctuations and resist emotional decision-making.

Traders pursuing short-term strategies should invest time honing their technical analysis skills, understanding chart patterns, and familiarizing themselves with indicators. Effective risk management, discipline, and the ability to control emotions are essential for successful short-term traders.

The choice between long-term and short-term strategies in altcoin investing is not binary; it exists along a spectrum. Some investors blend elements of both strategies, holding a core portfolio of promising altcoins while engaging in short-term trades to capture price fluctuations.

Regardless of the selected strategy, it is essential to approach altcoin investing holistically. Diversification, thorough research, disciplined risk management, and a resilient mindset are vital to any successful approach. The altcoin market is a dynamic arena with transformative potential, and both long-term investors and short-term traders contribute to the ecosystem's growth and evolution.

Ultimately, the journey through the altcoin landscape is a testament to investors' diverse strategies to navigate innovation, volatility, and opportunity. By understanding the nuances of long-term and short-term approaches, individuals can forge a path that aligns with their financial goals, risk appetite, and vision for the evolving world of cryptocurrency.

CHAPTER V

Promising Altcoins and Emerging Crypto Projects

In-depth analysis of select altcoins with strong potential

In the expansive universe of cryptocurrencies, altcoins stand as a testament to innovation, offering a diverse array of projects beyond the towering presence of Bitcoin. As the cryptocurrency ecosystem evolves, certain altcoins have emerged as beacons of promise, captivating the attention of investors and enthusiasts alike. These select altcoins exhibit compelling use cases, technological innovations, and visionary development teams that position them for potential growth in a rapidly changing landscape. In this section, we explore several altcoins with strong potential in-depth, uncovering the intricacies of their technology, applications, and market positioning.

Ethereum, often dubbed the "world computer," has transcended its status as an altcoin to become a foundational platform for decentralized applications (dApps) and smart contracts. Ethereum established the idea of programmable blockchains and is supported by its native cryptocurrency Ether (ETH), which enables developers to establish a wide variety of applications on its platform. Ethereum's success lies in its ability to facilitate self-executing smart contracts, which automate processes without intermediaries.

Ethereum's strong potential stems from its robust ecosystem, which includes a plethora of dApps spanning finance, gaming, decentralized finance (DeFi), non-fungible tokens (NFTs), and more. Its upgrade to Ethereum 2.0 aims to enhance scalability and energy efficiency, addressing long-standing concerns about high transaction fees and network congestion.

Cardano is an altcoin project that prioritizes scientific research, peer-reviewed development, and sustainability. Driven by its native cryptocurrency ADA, Cardano aims to create a blockchain ecosystem that balances technological innovation with rigorous academic scrutiny. Its unique approach involves multiple development phases, each introducing incremental improvements to enhance security, scalability, and interoperability.

Cardano's potential is underscored by its focus on solving real-world problems. It aims to enable financial inclusion in underserved regions by partnering with governments and institutions. With its emphasis on research-driven development and compliance with regulatory standards, Cardano presents a compelling case for long-term viability.

Solana has emerged as a formidable contender in the altcoin arena, addressing the scalability limitations that have plagued other blockchain networks. By utilizing a unique consensus mechanism known as Proof of History (PoH), Solana achieves high throughput and low latency, making it well-suited for applications like decentralized finance (DeFi) and non-fungible tokens (NFTs).

The strength of Solana's potential resides in its capacity to draw projects and developers looking for a platform that can manage high transaction volumes without compromising speed. Its ecosystem includes various DeFi protocols, NFT marketplaces, and gaming platforms, positioning it as a key player in shaping the future of blockchain applications.

Polygon, formerly known as Matic Network, addresses one of the most pressing challenges facing the Ethereum network: scalability. Acting as a layer 2 solution, Polygon enhances Ethereum's throughput and reduces transaction fees by enabling faster and cheaper transactions on its sidechain.

Polygon's potential stems from its compatibility with Ethereum, allowing users to move assets between the two networks seamlessly. Its ecosystem boasts a range of dApps, DeFi platforms, and NFT projects, benefiting from the enhanced scalability provided by its layer 2 architecture.

Polkadot introduces a novel approach to blockchain interoperability, enabling different blockchains to communicate and share information seamlessly. Founded by Ethereum co-founder Dr. Gavin Wood, Polkadot seeks to establish a network of interconnected blockchains that can collaborate while maintaining their independence.

Polkadot's potential lies in fostering collaboration and innovation across disparate blockchain networks. Its parachain architecture enables specialized blockchains to connect to the Polkadot network, creating a versatile ecosystem that accommodates various use cases and projects.

Avalanche is an altcoin project that reimagines consensus mechanisms, aiming to combine the benefits of proof of work and proof of stake approaches. The project achieves high security and fast transaction confirmation times by introducing the Avalanche consensus protocol, making it suitable for various applications.

Avalanche's potential is rooted in its ability to support complex applications while maintaining decentralization. Its platform caters to DeFi, enterprise solutions, and NFTs, positioning it as a versatile contender in the altcoin landscape.

The altcoin landscape is a realm of infinite possibility characterized by technological breakthroughs, visionary projects, and transformative potential. Despite the fact that the aforementioned altcoins have great potential, it is important to recognize that the cryptocurrency market is dynamic and prone to volatility, legislative changes, and technological improvements.

Investors and enthusiasts exploring the altcoin frontier should approach their journey with diligence, research, and a discerning mindset. Thoroughly understanding each altcoin's technology, use cases, development team, and market positioning is essential for making informed decisions.

As the altcoin ecosystem continues to evolve, the projects highlighted in this essay exemplify the innovation, ambition, and potential that define this vibrant space. Through careful analysis and strategic engagement, investors and enthusiasts contribute to shaping the future of finance, technology, and decentralized possibilities.

Case studies of successful altcoin projects

In the ever-expanding landscape of cryptocurrencies, altcoins have risen to prominence as innovative contenders beyond the dominance of Bitcoin. These alternative digital assets offer a canvas of possibilities, from decentralized finance (DeFi) to non-fungible tokens (NFTs) and more. As the altcoin ecosystem continues to evolve, specific projects have carved a niche for themselves, capturing the attention of investors, developers, and users alike. In this section, we delve into case studies of successful altcoin projects, uncovering the factors contributing to their triumphs and examining the lessons they offer for the broader cryptocurrency landscape.

Binance Coin, launched by the Binance exchange in 2017, is a prime example of an altcoin that has achieved remarkable success through utility and innovation. Initially created as a utility token to pay for trading fees on the Binance platform, BNB has since expanded its use cases to include participation in token sales, payment for services, and even powering Binance Smart Chain (BSC), a blockchain platform for decentralized applications.

BNB's success can be attributed to its close integration with one of the world's largest cryptocurrency exchanges, Binance. The token's utility within the exchange's ecosystem and its strategic expansion into DeFi and NFT spaces through BSC has positioned BNB as a versatile and valuable altcoin project.

Chainlink has emerged as a leader in providing decentralized oracles that enable smart contracts to interact with real-world data securely. Launched in 2017, Chainlink addresses a critical limitation of smart contracts—their inability to access external information beyond the blockchain. By facilitating data connectivity, Chainlink enables smart contracts to execute based on real-time information, opening the door to many use cases across industries.

Chainlink's success lies in its pragmatic application of blockchain technology to real-world problems. Its decentralized oracle network enhances the reliability and accuracy of data inputs for smart contracts, thus expanding the potential applications of blockchain technology beyond the realm of cryptocurrencies.

Uniswap, a decentralized exchange (DEX) built on the Ethereum blockchain, exemplifies the transformative potential of decentralized finance (DeFi). Uniswap allows users to trade cryptocurrencies without intermediaries, relying on smart contracts and liquidity pools to facilitate trades. Its automated market-making (AMM) mechanism ensures continuous liquidity and efficient price discovery.

Uniswap's success can be attributed to its user-friendly interface, low barriers to entry, and role in democratizing access to DeFi services. It empowers users to participate in trading and liquidity provision while circumventing the limitations and risks associated with traditional centralized exchanges.

Aave, a DeFi protocol, has redefined the landscape of lending and borrowing within the cryptocurrency ecosystem. Operating on the Ethereum blockchain, Aave enables users to lend and borrow various cryptocurrencies through smart contracts. It includes features like flash loans, which let users borrow assets without providing any kind of collateral for as long as the loan is repaid in the same transaction.

Aave's success can be attributed to its innovative approach to borrowing and lending. Its integration of flash loans, diverse collateral options, and interest rate customization empowers users to engage in a more flexible and decentralized financial ecosystem.

Axie Infinity is a unique altcoin project that merges gaming and blockchain technology, tapping into the emerging trend of play-to-earn. On the Ethereum blockchain, Axie Infinity enables people to gather, reproduce, and engage in combat with "Axies," which are fictional creatures. Players can earn rewards through AXS tokens and other assets by participating in battles, breeding, and other in-game activities.

Axie Infinity's success is a testament to its ability to engage users through gamified incentives while leveraging blockchain to tokenize in-game assets. It taps into the growing demand for NFT-based gaming experiences, demonstrating the potential for innovative use cases that bridge the worlds of technology and entertainment.

The case studies of successful altcoin projects highlighted above underscore the diverse paths to success in the ever-evolving cryptocurrency landscape. These projects have demonstrated the significance of utility, innovation, user-centric design, and the ability to address real-world challenges.

While these successes provide valuable insights, it is essential to recognize that the altcoin ecosystem is characterized by rapid change, volatility, and unpredictability. The journey toward success has its challenges, regulatory considerations, and technological advancements that can impact even the most promising projects.

Investors, developers, and enthusiasts seeking to navigate the altcoin landscape should approach their endeavors with creativity, diligence, and adaptability. The lessons from successful altcoin projects illuminate the potential for transformative innovation that spans finance, technology, entertainment, and beyond.

The journey through the altcoin landscape is ultimately a testament to the seemingly limitless potential of human invention, as each initiative helps to determine the future of cryptocurrencies and blockchain technology. As the altcoin ecosystem evolves, these successful case studies serve as beacons of inspiration, guiding the way toward a future where innovation and opportunity intersect in dynamic harmony.

Upcoming ICOs and new project launches to watch

The world of cryptocurrencies is in a perpetual state of innovation, with new projects and initiatives continuously emerging to disrupt traditional paradigms and redefine industries. Initial Coin Offerings (ICOs) have historically been a popular method for fundraising and launching new projects within the cryptocurrency ecosystem. These ICOs, akin to Initial Public Offerings (IPOs) in traditional finance, allow investors to acquire tokens representing a stake in a project or platform. In this section, we delve into the realm of upcoming ICOs and new project launches to watch, exploring the factors that make these ventures compelling, their challenges, and the evolving landscape of token sales.

ICOs have played a pivotal role in expanding the cryptocurrency ecosystem, serving as a vital funding source for ambitious projects. These token sales enable startups and established players to secure capital and develop decentralized platforms, applications, and technologies.

ICOs are attractive for several reasons. They democratize investment, allowing retail investors to participate alongside institutional players. They also facilitate global fundraising, unburdened by geographical limitations. Moreover, successful ICOs provide investors with early access to potentially valuable tokens, incentivizing them to support projects aligned with their interests.

While ICOs offer a pathway for innovation, they are not without challenges. Regulatory uncertainty, fraudulent projects, and a lack of investor protection have previously marred the ICO landscape. Regulatory bodies worldwide have grappled with classifying tokens as securities, commodities, or utility tokens, adding complexity to the legal framework governing ICOs.

In response to these challenges, the landscape of token sales has evolved. Security Token Offerings (STOs) emerged as an attempt to introduce regulatory compliance and investor protections to the token sale process. Initial Exchange Offerings (IEOs) further streamlined the process by hosting token sales directly on cryptocurrency exchanges.

Numerous upcoming ICOs and new project launches warrant attention as the cryptocurrency ecosystem evolves. One such project is Polkadot. Led by Dr. Gavin Wood, co-founder of Ethereum, Polkadot seeks to establish a network of interoperable blockchains, enabling seamless communication and collaboration between different blockchain networks.

Another project to watch is Algorand, a platform that focuses on improving blockchain technology's scalability, security, and efficiency. Algorand employs a consensus mechanism that ensures transaction decentralization, scalability, and immediate finality.

Filecoin is also garnering attention as a decentralized storage network that aims to revolutionize data storage and access. It makes use of a marketplace built on the blockchain to let users rent out any extra storage space and receive Filecoin tokens in exchange.

Additionally, Elrond is emerging as a project that focuses on providing fast and cost-effective blockchain solutions. With a unique Adaptive State Sharding mechanism, Elrond aims to scale blockchain networks while maintaining security and decentralization.

Upcoming ICOs and new project launches promise to drive innovation, foster decentralization, and reshape traditional industries. However, investors must approach these opportunities with discernment and due diligence. Conducting thorough research on the project's technology, team, use case, and regulatory compliance is paramount.

Regulatory uncertainties persist in ICOs, highlighting the importance of projects adhering to legal frameworks and investor protection mechanisms. Projects prioritizing compliance as the regulatory landscape matures are better positioned for long-term success.

While ICOs have paved the way for innovation, they are part of a broader evolution in token sales. STOs, IEOs, and alternative fundraising models continue to shape the landscape. Investors, developers, and enthusiasts must remain vigilant in navigating this ever-changing terrain.

The world of cryptocurrencies remains a realm of boundless potential, where groundbreaking ideas have the power to transform industries and reshape economies. Upcoming ICOs and new project launches represent the vanguard of this innovation, inviting participants to engage, invest, and contribute to a future that blurs the boundaries between technology, finance, and human ingenuity.

Trends in altcoin development and adoption

The cryptocurrency landscape is in a perpetual evolution, with altcoins continuously pushing the boundaries of innovation and adoption. Altcoins, or alternative cryptocurrencies to Bitcoin, represent various projects that harness blockchain technology for many use cases. As the space matures, distinct trends in altcoin development and adoption have emerged, reshaping industries, revolutionizing financial systems, and altering how we perceive value and trust. In this section, we delve into the prominent trends shaping the world of altcoin development and adoption, shedding light on their significance and potential implications for the future.

One of the most profound trends in altcoin development and adoption is the rise of decentralized finance (DeFi). DeFi projects aim to recreate traditional financial services such as lending, borrowing, trading, and yield farming in a decentralized, permissionless manner. Altcoins like Compound (COMP), Aave (AAVE), and MakerDAO (MKR) have pioneered this movement, enabling users to lend, borrow, and gain interest on their cryptocurrency holdings directly through smart contracts.

DeFi's rapid growth underscores the demand for financial services that transcend traditional intermediaries. As these altcoins gain adoption, they challenge conventional financial systems by offering greater accessibility, transparency, and control to users worldwide.

Non-fungible tokens (NFTs) represent another transformative trend within the altcoin ecosystem. NFTs are unique digital assets that prove ownership and authenticity of various digital and physical items, such as art, music, virtual real estate, and collectibles. Altcoins like CryptoKitties, Decentraland (MANA), and Enjin Coin (ENJ) have played pivotal roles in driving NFT adoption.

NFTs have disrupted industries ranging from art and entertainment to gaming and fashion. They have empowered creators to monetize their digital works while introducing new ways for users to interact with and own digital assets. As NFTs continue to gain traction, they challenge traditional notions of ownership and revolutionize content monetization.

Scalability has been a persistent challenge for blockchain networks, limiting their throughput and transaction speed. In response, the trend of layer 2 scalability solutions has emerged. Altcoins like Polygon (MATIC) and Optimism (OPT) introduce layer 2 solutions that operate alongside existing blockchains, enhancing their scalability and reducing congestion.

These altcoins leverage sidechains and rollup technologies to process transactions off-chain while maintaining security and interoperability. By addressing scalability concerns, layer 2 solutions pave the way for widespread use of blockchain technology by improving user experience and reducing transaction costs.

Interoperability—the ability of different blockchain networks to communicate and share information seamlessly—is a crucial trend in altcoin development. Altcoins like Polkadot (DOT) and Cosmos (ATOM) are at the forefront of developing interoperability solutions that enable different blockchains to collaborate and exchange value.

Interoperability unlocks opportunities for cross-chain asset transfers, shared liquidity, and enhanced functionality. As projects work toward bridging disparate blockchains, they create a more cohesive ecosystem that leverages the strengths of multiple networks.

As the environmental impact of blockchain networks gains attention, a trend toward environmentally conscious altcoin development has emerged. Projects like Cardano (ADA) and Solana (SOL) are making strides toward energy efficiency and sustainability.

These altcoins are exploring consensus mechanisms that consume less energy and developing solutions to minimize carbon footprints. The shift toward environmental responsibility aligns with broader efforts to ensure blockchain technology's long-term viability and ethical considerations.

Altcoins are increasingly facilitating the integration of real-world assets into the digital realm. Projects like Wrapped Bitcoin (WBTC) and Terra (LUNA) enable tokenizing traditional assets such as fiat currencies, commodities, and stocks.

By bridging the gap between digital and tangible assets, these altcoins create opportunities for fractional ownership, increased liquidity, and borderless transfers of value. This trend has the potential to reshape the financial landscape by digitizing traditional assets and democratizing access to them.

While not traditional altcoins, central bank digital currencies (CBDCs) represent a significant trend within the cryptocurrency ecosystem. Countries like China, Sweden, and the Bahamas have launched or are piloting CBDCs to digitize their national currencies.

CBDCs blur the lines between traditional fiat currencies and cryptocurrencies, offering benefits such as faster transactions, reduced costs, and increased financial inclusion. As CBDCs gain traction, they introduce new dynamics to the global financial system and potentially influence the development of private-sector altcoins.

The trends shaping altcoin development and adoption reflect the rapid evolution of blockchain technology and its expanding impact on various industries. From DeFi to NFTs, layer 2 solutions to interoperability, altcoins are redefining financial systems, transforming creative sectors, and offering novel ways to interact with digital assets.

As these trends gain momentum, they present both opportunities and challenges. Altcoin developers must balance innovation with responsible governance, user privacy with regulatory compliance, and technological advancements with environmental considerations. Similarly, investors and users must exercise diligence and discernment as they navigate the diverse altcoin landscape.

The altcoin ecosystem is a testament to blockchain technology's potential to revolutionize how we interact, transact, and create value. As trends continue to emerge and evolve, altcoins will be pivotal in shaping the future of finance, technology, and human collaboration.

CHAPTER VI

Navigating the ICO and Token Sale Landscape

Understanding Initial Coin Offerings (ICOs) and token sales

The evolution of blockchain technology has given birth to Bitcoin and a myriad of innovative projects seeking to harness its potential for transformative change. Among the methods of funding these projects, Initial Coin Offerings (ICOs) have gained prominence as a groundbreaking approach to raising capital in the digital age. ICOs, often referred to as token sales, provide a means for startups and established players alike to access funding while democratizing investment opportunities and fueling the growth of new decentralized ecosystems. In this section, we delve into the intricacies of ICOs and token sales, exploring their significance, mechanics, regulatory challenges, and potential implications for the future of finance and technology.

The paradigm of fundraising has changed, and initial coin offerings (ICOs) are a blockchain-based substitute for conventional funding techniques like venture capital and also initial public offerings (IPOs). A project that participates in an ICO essentially sells a new cryptocurrency, referred to as a token, to the public in return for more well-known ones like Bitcoin (also known as BTC) or Ethereum (also known as ETH). These tokens, which represent digital assets that can be used for a variety of reasons, such as accessing services, taking part in governance, or even representing ownership of underlying assets, frequently have unique utility inside the project's ecosystem.

Token sales, a broader term encompassing ICOs, also include Security Token Offerings (STOs), which involve tokens that represent ownership in traditional assets like equities or real estate. This distinction is crucial in understanding the regulatory landscape, as STOs are often subject to securities regulations.

The journey of an ICO begins with the creation of a detailed whitepaper. This document outlines the project's vision, technology, use cases, tokenomics (token economics), development timeline, and the problems the project aims to solve. The whitepaper serves as a blueprint for potential investors to evaluate the project's feasibility and align their interests.

Once the whitepaper is published, the project launches a token sale event. During this event, investors purchase tokens with established cryptocurrencies, providing the project with the capital needed for development. The tokens are then distributed to investors' wallets after the token sale concludes.

ICOs may include multiple stages, such as private sales, presales, and public sales, each with varying terms, discounts, and lock-up periods. These stages cater to different categories of investors and often prioritize early supporters or strategic partners.

ICOs have traversed a complex regulatory landscape since their inception. Regulatory bodies worldwide grapple with classifying tokens as securities, commodities, or utility tokens, which has significant implications for legal compliance and investor protection.

Projects implementing ICOs must traverse this complex terrain of differing securities laws to ensure compliance with securities legislation. Failure to do so may have legal implications, such as fines and the need to return investment funds.

The emergence of STOs, which explicitly involve securities, has led to attempts to introduce regulatory compliance and investor protections into token sales. These efforts aim to close the gap between blockchain technology and traditional financial frameworks.

The ICO boom of 2017 brought significant attention and investment to the cryptocurrency space. However, it also led to fraudulent projects, overhyped promises, and a lack of due diligence by investors and project teams. This led to a subsequent market correction, known as the "ICO bubble burst," which resulted in many projects' token values declining.

The ICO bubble burst is a crucial lesson in the importance of thorough research, realistic expectations, and regulatory adherence. It underscored the need for projects to focus on genuine technological innovation, sustainable business models, and transparent communication.

As the cryptocurrency ecosystem evolves, the landscape of token sales has transformed. Initial Exchange Offerings (IEOs) emerged as a response to regulatory uncertainties and the need for a more secure fundraising method. IEOs involve cryptocurrency exchanges hosting token sales on their platforms, vetting projects and providing a streamlined user experience for investors.

Security Token Offerings (STOs) introduced the concept of regulated token sales, combining the benefits of blockchain technology with the investor protections provided by traditional securities laws. STOs represent a bridge between the old and new worlds of finance, offering a compliant pathway for traditional assets to be digitized and traded on blockchain networks.

Furthermore, the emergence of Central Bank Digital Currencies (CBDCs) adds a new layer to the evolving landscape. As governments explore digitizing their national currencies, they enter the realm of token issuance, blurring the lines between conventional fiat currencies and cryptocurrencies.

ICOs and token sales represent a transformative shift in how projects access capital, investors engage with projects, and traditional financial paradigms are challenged. These innovative funding methods have democratized investment opportunities, enabled global participation, and accelerated the development of decentralized ecosystems.

However, the journey of ICOs and token sales has been marked by challenges, from regulatory uncertainties to fraudulent schemes. The lessons learned from these experiences are essential as the cryptocurrency ecosystem moves forward with more regulated and sophisticated models like STOs and CBDCs.

The intersection of blockchain technology, finance, and decentralization is reshaping the future of capital markets. ICOs and token sales have laid the foundation for this transformation, offering a glimpse into a world where innovation, accessibility, and financial inclusion converge. As the cryptocurrency landscape continues to evolve, the journey of ICOs and token sales remains integral to the broader narrative, carving the path toward a new era of finance and technology.

Evaluating ICO whitepapers: What to look for

Initial Coin Offerings (ICOs) have appeared as a revolutionary method for funding innovative projects in the dynamic landscape of blockchain and cryptocurrency. At the heart of each ICO is the whitepaper—a comprehensive document that outlines the project's vision, technology, use cases, tokenomics, and more. Evaluating ICO whitepapers is crucial for investors and enthusiasts to make informed decisions in a space characterized by rapid innovation and potential pitfalls. In this section, we delve into the essential elements to look for when evaluating ICO whitepapers, highlighting the significance of each aspect in understanding a project's feasibility, value proposition, and potential for success.

A robust whitepaper begins by articulating the project's vision and the real-world problem it aims to solve. This section should provide a clear and concise overview of the project's purpose, demonstrating an understanding of the market gap or challenge it seeks to address. The problem statement is the foundation upon which the entire project is built, ensuring its meaningful impact and relevance.

The heart of any blockchain project lies in its technological innovation. Investors should carefully assess the technical aspects described in the whitepaper, such as the consensus mechanism, scalability solutions, interoperability, and security measures. Projects introducing novel solutions to existing challenges or leveraging innovative consensus mechanisms are more likely to stand out in a competitive landscape.

Tokenomics refers to the economic model that underpins the project's token. In this section, the whitepaper should explain how the token will be used within the ecosystem, detailing its utility, distribution, and potential for value appreciation. A well-designed tokenomics model ensures that the token has a clear purpose, drives ecosystem growth, and aligns incentives for all stakeholders.

The roadmap outlines the project's milestones, goals, and anticipated timeline for development. It provides a glimpse into the project's progression and sets expectations for deliverables. A comprehensive and well-defined roadmap demonstrates that the project team has a strategic plan and is committed to achieving its objectives.

The credentials and expertise of the project's team members are crucial indicators of the project's potential for success. Whitepapers should introduce the key team members, highlighting their relevant experience and accomplishments in the blockchain and relevant industries. Additionally, the involvement of respected advisors or partners can enhance the project's credibility and increase investor confidence.

A thorough market analysis demonstrates that the project team deeply understands the industry landscape and its potential for disruption. This section should provide insights into market trends, target demographics, and potential competitors. Projects strategically positioned within a broader ecosystem are better equipped to capture market share.

Regulatory compliance is a critical aspect of ICO whitepapers. Investors should look for clear statements regarding the project's legal status, adherence to local regulations, and measures in place to ensure compliance.

Projects demonstrating a proactive approach to regulatory challenges are more likely to successfully navigate the ever-evolving legal landscape.

A thriving community often indicates a project's potential for adoption and growth. Whitepapers should detail the project's engagement strategy, including plans for user acquisition, partnerships, and ecosystem development. Strong community support can contribute to the project's success by driving adoption and facilitating network effects.

Transparency is crucial in the evaluation of an ICO. The whitepaper should provide comprehensive and accurate information and clearly explain technical concepts. Furthermore, the project team's commitment to ongoing communication and updates is essential for maintaining investor trust and confidence.

A well-rounded whitepaper acknowledges potential risks and uncertainties associated with the project. It should outline the key risks—technological, regulatory, market-related, etc.—and provide mitigation strategies demonstrating the project team's preparedness and ability to navigate challenges.

Evaluating ICO whitepapers requires analytical thinking, technical understanding, and due diligence. Investors and enthusiasts must look beyond flashy marketing and promises to critically assess the project's feasibility, value proposition, and potential for long-term success. By focusing on the aspects discussed in this essay—project vision, technological innovation, tokenomics, team expertise, market analysis, regulatory compliance, community engagement, and more—individuals can make well-informed decisions contributing to the growth and maturation of the blockchain and cryptocurrency ecosystem.

ICOs have revolutionized how projects raise capital and engage with a global audience. However, the absence of regulatory oversight and the potential for fraudulent schemes highlight the importance of thorough evaluation. By honing the skill of critically analyzing ICO whitepapers, investors and enthusiasts play an active role in shaping the trajectory of blockchain projects, contributing to creating a sustainable and innovative digital future.

Due diligence before investing in ICOs

As the world of blockchain and cryptocurrencies continues to evolve, Initial Coin Offerings (ICOs) have emerged as a prominent method for fundraising and investment. ICOs offer a unique opportunity for individuals to participate in early-stage projects that leverage blockchain technology to disrupt industries and create innovative solutions. However, with this opportunity comes a set of challenges and risks. Due diligence before investing in ICOs is crucial to make informed decisions, mitigate risks, and ensure the safety of investments. In this section, we delve into the intricacies of conducting due diligence before investing in ICOs, exploring the steps, considerations, and best practices that can empower investors to navigate the complex landscape of token sales.

Before delving into the technical details, it's essential to grasp the fundamental concept and purpose of the project. Investigate the project's website, whitepaper, and any available documentation to understand its vision, goals, and value proposition. Ensure that the project's objectives align with your investment preferences and values.

The team behind an ICO is a critical factor in assessing the project's potential for success. Research the backgrounds, expertise, and track records of key team members. Evaluate their experience in the blockchain space, relevant industries, and their ability to execute the project's vision. A credible and capable team increases the project's likelihood of achieving its goals.

Scrutinize the tokenomics model outlined in the whitepaper. Understand how the tokens will be used within the ecosystem, their utility, and their potential for appreciation. Investigate whether the tokens serve a functional purpose within the project or if they are merely speculative assets. Projects with clear and well-defined token use cases tend to have more sustainable growth potential.

Dive into the technical aspects of the project's blockchain technology. Assess the technology's novelty, the proposed scalability solutions, and the project's differentiation from existing platforms. A strong technical foundation is crucial for long-term viability and adoption.

Conduct an in-depth analysis of the market the project aims to disrupt. Understand the target audience, potential competitors, and the project's competitive advantage. A comprehensive understanding of the market landscape helps assess the project's potential for adoption and growth.

Ensure that the project adheres to regulatory guidelines in its jurisdiction. Projects demonstrating a proactive approach to compliance and legal considerations are more likely to navigate regulatory challenges successfully.

Investigate whether the project's token can be classified as a security and whether it complies with securities regulations.

Evaluate the project's engagement with its community. Check its presence on social media platforms, online forums, and communication channels. An active and engaged community indicates a higher level of interest and support, which can contribute to the project's success.

Assess the project's transparency and communication efforts. A transparent project team that provides regular updates, addresses concerns, and engages with the community fosters trust and confidence among investors. Look for projects that prioritize open communication and share progress reports.

Analyze the project's roadmap and development timeline. Check whether the milestones are realistic and achievable. A well-defined roadmap demonstrates that the project team has a clear strategy and is committed to delivering on its promises.

Seek out independent reviews and analyst insights on the project. Trusted blockchain and cryptocurrency experts often provide valuable assessments of ICOs, highlighting strengths, weaknesses, and potential risks.

Be vigilant for red flags that indicate potential scams or fraudulent projects. High returns with minimal risk, lack of transparency, overly aggressive marketing, and unverified team members are all warning signs that require careful consideration.

Consider the size of your investment and ensure that it aligns with your risk tolerance. Diversify your investments over different projects to spread risk and minimize potential losses.

The process of due diligence before investing in ICOs is a comprehensive and meticulous undertaking. It requires research skills, technical understanding, and critical thinking. By thoroughly evaluating the project's concept, team, tokenomics, technology, market, compliance, community engagement, and communication efforts, investors can make knowledgeable decisions that contribute to the growth and maturation of the blockchain ecosystem.

Investing in ICOs offers the potential for significant returns, but it also carries inherent risks. The absence of regulatory oversight and the possibility of fraudulent projects emphasize the importance of conducting thorough due diligence. By following the steps and considerations outlined in this section, investors can confidently approach ICO investments, maximize their chances of success, and actively contribute to advancing innovative blockchain projects. In a landscape characterized by innovation and volatility, due diligence serves as a guiding light, empowering investors to navigate the complexities of ICOs and make investments that align with their financial goals and aspirations.

Regulatory changes impacting ICOs and token sales

The intersection of blockchain technology and finance has ushered in a new era of innovation, revolutionizing industries and reshaping traditional paradigms. Within this landscape, Initial Coin Offerings (ICOs) and token sales have emerged as powerful fundraising mechanisms that leverage the potential of decentralized networks. However, the rapid rise of ICOs has prompted regulatory bodies worldwide to scrutinize these novel methods of capital formation, resulting in a dynamic and evolving regulatory environment. In this section, we explore the regulatory changes impacting ICOs and token sales, delving into the reasons behind regulatory scrutiny, the challenges posed by varying global approaches, and the potential implications for the future of blockchain-based fundraising.

Regulatory authorities have turned their attention to ICOs and token sales due to concerns surrounding investor protection, market integrity, money laundering, and potential risks to financial stability. These fundraising mechanisms' decentralized and cross-border nature poses unique challenges to traditional regulatory frameworks. The absence of intermediaries, coupled with the global accessibility of ICOs, has raised questions about jurisdiction, legal status, and the need for regulatory clarity.

The regulatory response to ICOs and token sales varies significantly from one jurisdiction to another. Some countries have embraced these innovations, recognizing their potential to drive economic growth and technological advancement. Other jurisdictions have taken a more cautious stance, citing concerns about fraud, speculative bubbles, and the lack of investor safeguards.

This divergence in regulatory approaches has created a complex landscape for projects and investors. While some countries provide clear guidelines for token sales, others impose outright bans or operate within a gray area where the regulatory status remains uncertain.

One of the central challenges in regulating ICOs revolves around the classification of tokens. Tokens can be broadly categorized as security tokens, utility tokens, or a hybrid of both. Security tokens represent ownership interests in a company and are subject to securities regulations. Utility tokens, on the other hand, grant access to a product or service within a decentralized network and may not be considered securities.

Regulatory authorities grapple with determining whether a token falls under the definition of a security and is subject to securities laws. The distinction has significant implications for compliance, investor protection, and the obligations of project teams.

To address the challenges posed by ICOs and token sales, various countries and international bodies have introduced regulatory frameworks or guidelines. The United States, for example, employs the "Howey Test" to determine if a token qualifies as a security. The European Union has taken a more nuanced approach, evaluating tokens case-by-case. Meanwhile, some countries, like Switzerland, have introduced principles-based frameworks that provide regulatory certainty while accommodating innovation.

Efforts to strike a balance between fostering innovation and safeguarding investors are ongoing. Regulatory sandboxes, where projects can operate under controlled conditions, have been proposed to test new ideas while ensuring compliance with regulatory requirements.

The evolving regulatory landscape has profoundly impacted ICOs and token sales. Regulatory uncertainty can deter projects from launching token sales, particularly in jurisdictions with ambiguous or restrictive guidelines. Investors, too, may be cautious about participating in token sales that lack regulatory clarity, as legal and financial risks remain a concern.

While regulatory scrutiny can introduce challenges, it can also foster greater transparency and accountability within the industry. Projects prioritizing compliance and investor protection may gain a competitive advantage, ultimately contributing to the maturation and legitimacy of the blockchain ecosystem.

As the blockchain industry matures, the importance of regulatory clarity cannot be overstated. Industry participants, regulatory bodies, and policymakers must collaborate to establish clear guidelines that protect investors, encourage innovation, and maintain market integrity. Regulatory sandboxes, pilot programs, and open dialogue between stakeholders can facilitate the development of effective regulatory frameworks that balance innovation and compliance.

International cooperation is also crucial in addressing the global nature of ICOs and token sales. Cross-border projects necessitate harmonization of regulatory approaches to avoid regulatory arbitrage and make a level playing field for market participants.

Amidst the changing regulatory landscape, education is vital. Projects, investors, and the broader community must educate themselves about the regulatory requirements in their jurisdiction. Seeking legal advice, understanding the implications of different token classifications, and conducting thorough due diligence before participating in ICOs are essential for navigating the evolving regulatory environment.

The regulatory changes impacting ICOs and token sales reflect the delicate balance between encouraging innovation and safeguarding investors. As blockchain technology continues to disrupt traditional models, it challenges regulatory norms and prompts a reevaluation of existing frameworks.

The global nature of ICOs calls for collaborative efforts among stakeholders to establish clear and comprehensive regulatory guidelines. The blockchain ecosystem can navigate the uncertainty and complexity of regulatory changes by fostering a dialogue between projects, investors, regulatory bodies, and policymakers.

While regulatory challenges persist, they also allow the industry to mature, evolve, and build a foundation of trust and transparency. The resilience and adaptability demonstrated by the blockchain community in response to regulatory changes will be pivotal in shaping the future of ICOs, token sales, and the broader adoption of blockchain technology.

CHAPTER VII

The Role of Altcoins in a Decentralized Future

Altcoins as catalysts for innovation in blockchain technology

The appearance of Bitcoin in 2009 marked the beginning of a revolutionary journey that has reshaped the world of finance, technology, and human collaboration. While Bitcoin's pioneering role in introducing the concept of decentralized digital currency cannot be overstated, it also paved the way for the development of alternative cryptocurrencies, often referred to as altcoins. Altcoins, short for "alternative coins," encompass diverse blockchain-based digital assets beyond Bitcoin. These altcoins have become vehicles for diversification and investment and powerful catalysts for innovation in blockchain technology. In this section, we delve into the profound impact of altcoins as catalysts for innovation, exploring their role in driving technological advancements, fostering competition, and shaping the future trajectory of blockchain ecosystems.

While Bitcoin introduced the concept of a decentralized ledger and digital scarcity, altcoins have embraced technological diversity and experimentation. Ethereum, for instance, introduced the idea of smart contracts and decentralized applications (dApps), allowing developers to create programmable blockchain-based solutions. This innovation inspired the development of numerous altcoins that explored different consensus mechanisms, scalability solutions, privacy enhancements, and governance models. The result is a dynamic ecosystem where altcoins serve as testbeds for groundbreaking technological advancements.

Bitcoin's scalability limitations and slow transaction speeds prompted the exploration of alternative consensus mechanisms and scaling solutions. Altcoins like Litecoin (LTC) introduced faster block confirmation times, while Nano (NANO) showcased the potential of fee-less and instant transactions. Other altcoins, such as Ripple (XRP) and Stellar (XLM), have focused on facilitating cross-border payments and remittances. These innovations have expanded the utility of blockchain technology and motivated further research and development in pursuit of scalable and efficient solutions.

Altcoins have also driven innovation in privacy and security features. Projects like Monero (XMR) and Zcash (ZEC) introduced advanced cryptographic techniques allowing private and confidential transactions. These privacy-focused altcoins address concerns surrounding transaction traceability and enhance user anonymity. As privacy becomes an increasingly important consideration in the digital age, these innovations have implications beyond cryptocurrencies and extend to broader discussions of data protection and personal sovereignty.

Decentralized Finance, or DeFi, represents one of the most transformative innovations in the blockchain space, and altcoins have played a pivotal role in its development. Altcoins like MakerDAO (MKR) and Compound (COMP) pioneered the concept of lending, borrowing, and earning interest through smart contracts. The DeFi movement has since grown to encompass various financial services, including decentralized exchanges, yield farming, and synthetic assets. The development of DeFi is still being driven by altcoins, which are democratizing the accessibility of financial services and posing a threat to established financial intermediaries.

As the blockchain ecosystem expands, the need for interoperability between different blockchains has become increasingly evident. Altcoins like Polkadot (DOT) and Cosmos (ATOM) have introduced solutions that facilitate communication and value transfer between disparate blockchains. These projects aim to create a more interconnected and seamless blockchain landscape, enabling the efficient exchange of assets and data across multiple networks.

Altcoins have also paved the way for tokenizing real-world assets, bringing traditional assets onto the blockchain. Projects like Terra (LUNA) and Synthetix (SNX) enable the creation of synthetic assets that mirror the value of real-world assets including fiat currencies, commodities, and stocks. This innovation can potentially democratize access to traditional financial markets and increase liquidity through fractional ownership.

Altcoins have introduced innovative governance models that empower token holders to participate in decision-making processes. The concept of Decentralized Autonomous Organizations (DAOs) leverages blockchain technology to create self-governing entities that make collective decisions through token-based voting. Altcoins like Tezos (XTZ) and Aragon (ANT) have pioneered this concept, enabling communities to manage and govern the development and evolution of projects collaboratively.

As environmental concerns gain prominence, altcoins are exploring energy-efficient consensus mechanisms as alternatives to the resource-intensive Proof of Work (PoW) model used by Bitcoin. Altcoins like Cardano (ADA) and Solana (SOL) are transitioning to Proof of Stake (PoS) or hybrid PoW/PoS models, significantly reducing energy consumption and environmental impact. These innovations highlight the adaptability of altcoins in addressing sustainability challenges.

Some altcoins have expanded the concept of tokenization beyond financial assets. Projects like Basic Attention Token (BAT) and Chiliz (CHZ) are tokenizing intellectual property, enabling content creators and sports teams to monetize their work and engage with their audiences directly.

Altcoins have emerged as pioneers of technological advancement within the blockchain space. Their innovative solutions, diverse use cases, and commitment to pushing the boundaries of what is possible have reshaped how we perceive technology, finance, and human collaboration. By fostering competition, experimenting with new consensus mechanisms, and addressing scalability, privacy, and governance challenges, altcoins have elevated the blockchain ecosystem to new heights.

As altcoins continue to evolve, their influence on blockchain technology will persist. Their role as catalysts for innovation ensures that the blockchain space remains dynamic, adaptive, and responsive to the ever-changing demands of a rapidly evolving digital landscape. As investors and enthusiasts engage with altcoins, they actively contribute to the ongoing narrative of blockchain innovation, fostering a future shaped by decentralized technologies' transformative potential.

Interoperability between different altcoins and blockchain networks

Once characterized by isolated and siloed networks, the blockchain landscape has undergone a significant evolution driven by the quest for enhanced functionality, scalability, and user experience. Interoperability, the ability of different blockchain networks and altcoins to communicate, share data, and collaborate seamlessly, has emerged as a critical concept in the blockchain ecosystem. While Bitcoin introduced the groundbreaking potential of decentralized digital currency, and Ethereum pioneered smart contracts and decentralized applications (dApps), the limitations of these individual networks led to the realization that true innovation lies in the collaboration and interconnection of diverse blockchain platforms. This section delves into the profound impact of interoperability between different altcoins and blockchain networks, exploring its importance, challenges, technological approaches, and the potential for a more connected and unified decentralized future.

The siloed nature of blockchain networks presents challenges in terms of scalability, efficiency, and usability. As the blockchain ecosystem expands, the need to enable value transfer, data exchange, and collaboration across different networks becomes increasingly apparent. Interoperability addresses these challenges by allowing diverse blockchain platforms to communicate and share information seamlessly, enhancing the overall functionality and utility of the technology. In essence, interoperability opens the door to a new era of collaboration, where the sum of various networks' capabilities exceeds the potential of any single network.

While the vision of interoperability is promising, achieving it is challenging. The diversity of consensus mechanisms, cryptographic algorithms, and technical architectures across various blockchain networks presents obstacles to seamless communication. Additionally, differing governance models, security considerations, and ideological differences among blockchain communities contribute to the complexity of interoperability efforts. These challenges highlight the need for standardized protocols and collaborative efforts to overcome technical barriers and establish a framework for interoperability.

Several technological approaches have been proposed to enable interoperability between different altcoins and blockchain networks. These approaches can be categorized into different layers of the technology stack:

Cross-Chain Communication Protocols: Atomic Swaps and Hashed TimeLock Contracts (HTLCs) enable the trustless exchange of assets between different blockchain networks. These protocols allow users to perform cross-chain swaps without intermediaries, facilitating direct peer-to-peer transactions across disparate networks.

Middleware Solutions: Middleware platforms like Polkadot and Cosmos aim to create a unified ecosystem by enabling different blockchains to connect and share information. In addition to facilitating the exchange of data and assets, these platforms add a layer of interoperability that enables the development of parachains—specialized blockchains that can communicate with the main chain.

Wrapped Tokens and Bridges: Wrapped tokens represent assets from one blockchain on another blockchain. Projects like Wrapped Bitcoin (WBTC) and Wrapped Ethereum (WETH) enable the tokenization of assets from one blockchain onto another, allowing them to be used within different ecosystems. On the other hand, Bridges facilitate the movement of assets between various networks by locking tokens on one chain and issuing equivalent tokens on another.

Decentralized Exchanges (DEXs): Some DEXs are built with cross-chain capabilities, allowing users to trade assets from different blockchains without centralized intermediaries. These cross-chain DEXs leverage technologies like atomic swaps to enable trustless and seamless trading between assets from various networks. Interledger Protocols: Interledger protocols like ILP facilitate payments and value transfer between different ledgers, enabling interoperability for financial transactions. These protocols provide a standardized framework for cross-chain payments and settlements.

Interoperability enables the transfer of value between different blockchain networks and facilitates collaboration between diverse ecosystems. DeFi protocols, for instance, can leverage interoperability to access liquidity from various blockchains, increasing the efficiency and composability of DeFi applications. Cross-chain dApps can also utilize interoperability to expand their user base and functionality by tapping into multiple networks. This ability to bridge different ecosystems enhances the overall utility of blockchain technology and fosters innovation across industries.

The quest for interoperability reflects the broader aspiration of creating a connected and unified decentralized ecosystem. The vision is to enable different blockchain networks to work together seamlessly, transcending geographical, technological, and ideological boundaries. A unified decentralized ecosystem holds the potential to drive innovation, enhance security through network diversity, and promote inclusivity by allowing users to access a wide range of services and applications. This interconnected ecosystem could pave the way for entirely novel use cases and applications that leverage the combined capabilities of different blockchains.

Achieving full interoperability remains a complex endeavor. Technical challenges, governance issues, and the need for standardized protocols are just a few of the considerations that must be addressed. Implementing interoperability solutions must also consider security, scalability, and the potential impact on network performance. Additionally, the trade-offs between decentralization, efficiency, and security must be carefully considered when designing cross-chain solutions.

While interoperability presents significant advantages, there is a need to balance collaboration and maintaining the unique strengths of individual blockchain networks. Each network has its characteristics, use cases, and governance models, and interoperability should enhance these qualities rather than homogenize them. Striking the right balance will ensure that interoperability preserves the diversity and innovation that the blockchain ecosystem thrives upon.

Collaborative efforts among different projects, communities, and developers mark the journey towards achieving interoperability. Open-source collaboration, standardization initiatives, and establishing interoperability-focused organizations are crucial in advancing the cause of a more connected blockchain ecosystem. Collaboration fosters the exchange of ideas, expertise, and resources needed to overcome technical challenges and provide comprehensive interoperability solutions.

Interoperability between different altcoins and blockchain networks represents a new era of collaboration and synergy within the blockchain space. As projects embrace the vision of a connected and unified decentralized ecosystem, they contribute to a future where blockchain technology transcends its current limitations and drives innovation on a global scale. The challenges and complexities of achieving interoperability are significant, but they are met with enthusiasm, determination, and a shared commitment to realizing the full potential of blockchain technology. As the blockchain landscape continues to evolve, interoperability stands as a testament to the power of collaboration and the boundless possibilities that lie ahead.

Altcoins in decentralized finance (DeFi) and non-fungible tokens (NFTs)

The expansion of blockchain technology has given rise to a diverse ecosystem of digital assets beyond traditional cryptocurrencies like Bitcoin. Altcoins, also known as alternative coins, have emerged as the building blocks of innovation, enabling the development of decentralized applications and novel use cases that extend beyond mere value transfer. Within this landscape, two prominent trends have gained remarkable traction: Decentralized Finance (DeFi) and Non-Fungible Tokens (NFTs). In this section, we explore the role of altcoins in both DeFi and NFTs, examining their contributions, challenges, and the transformative potential they hold for reshaping the financial landscape and the digital art world.

Decentralized Finance, or DeFi, represents a paradigm shift in how financial services are accessed and delivered. At the core of the DeFi movement are altcoins that provide the infrastructure for building decentralized applications and protocols. Ethereum, the second-largest cryptocurrency when it comes to market capitalization, has been a driving force in the DeFi space. Its versatile smart contract capabilities have enabled the creation of a wide range of DeFi platforms, including decentralized exchanges (DEXs), lending and borrowing protocols, stablecoins, and yield farming projects.

Beyond Ethereum, many altcoins have emerged to cater to specific DeFi use cases. Tokens like Chainlink (LINK) facilitate decentralized oracles, enabling the integration of real-world data into smart contracts. Synthetix (SNX) introduces synthetic assets that track real-world assets' value, opening doors to decentralized derivatives and trading. Aave (AAVE) and Compound (COMP) have revolutionized lending and borrowing in a trustless manner, empowering users to earn interest or borrow assets without intermediaries. The diversity of DeFi altcoins showcases the innovation fostered by blockchain's programmability.

Despite their transformative potential, DeFi altcoins face challenges that include scalability, security vulnerabilities, and the complexities of composability, where different protocols interact seamlessly. High gas fees on Ethereum have also driven the search for alternative blockchains with lower fees and greater scalability, leading to the growth of multi-chain DeFi solutions.

Non-Fungible Tokens (NFTs) represent a revolutionary concept in the digital art and collectibles space. Unlike fungible cryptocurrencies that are interchangeable, NFTs are unique and indivisible tokens representing ownership of a specific digital asset. Altcoins have played a pivotal role in enabling the NFT boom, providing platforms and ecosystems where NFTs can be created, traded, and utilized in various applications.

Blockchain platforms like Ethereum and Binance Smart Chain (BSC) have witnessed most NFT activity. Ethereum-based altcoins, such as ENJIN (ENJ) and Chiliz (CHZ), enable the creation of NFTs representing digital items in video games and sports, respectively. Altcoins also facilitate NFT marketplaces like OpenSea, where users can buy, sell, and trade NFTs, contributing to the growth of a digital collectibles economy.

NFTs have expanded beyond digital art and collectibles to encompass various applications. They are being used to tokenize real estate, represent ownership of virtual land in metaverse environments, and even authenticate physical assets using blockchain technology. Altcoins play a significant role in shaping the utility and use cases of NFTs, as each altcoin's features and capabilities influence the functionalities of the NFTs created on its platform.

While NFTs have garnered attention and adoption, challenges remain. Scalability concerns on Ethereum have led to congestion and high gas fees, impacting the accessibility of NFTs for mainstream users. Additionally, ensuring the security of NFT platforms and maintaining the long-term value of NFTs require continuous innovation and development.

The synergy between DeFi and NFTs is becoming increasingly evident. DeFi protocols have introduced mechanisms where users can use NFTs as collateral to access liquidity or earn yield. Integrating DeFi and NFTs blurs the lines between financial assets and collectibles, creating new opportunities for users to maximize the value of their digital possessions.

The intersection of altcoins, DeFi, and NFTs carries profound implications for finance, art, and beyond. DeFi's composability and NFTs' uniqueness are driving previously unimaginable innovations. Cross-chain solutions like Polkadot and Cosmos may facilitate the seamless interaction of diverse DeFi and NFT ecosystems, enhancing scalability and interoperability.

Altcoins are the driving force behind the transformative trends of DeFi and NFTs. Their programmability and diverse capabilities empower developers, creators, and users to envision and build decentralized financial systems and unique digital assets. As the DeFi ecosystem expands and NFTs find applications beyond art, altcoins continue to pave the way for a new digital era reshaping the boundaries of finance, art, ownership, and collaboration. The interaction between altcoins, DeFi, and NFTs is an excellent illustration of how blockchain technology may democratize the accessibility of financial services and give individuals new and creative power.

Shaping the future of the global financial system

The global financial landscape is undergoing a profound transformation, driven by the relentless innovation of blockchain technology and its most dynamic players: altcoins or alternative cryptocurrencies. While Bitcoin initiated the revolutionary concept of decentralized digital currency, altcoins have emerged as powerful agents of change that are redefining how we think about money, value transfer, and the very architecture of the financial system. In this section, we delve into the role of altcoins in shaping the future of the global financial system, exploring their impact on various aspects of finance, from remittances and cross-border transactions to banking services, financial inclusion, and the evolution of central bank digital currencies (CBDCs).

One of the most striking ways altcoins are shaping the financial future is by reimagining how remittances and cross-border transactions are conducted. Traditional methods are often slow, costly, and fraught with intermediaries. Altcoins, however, offer the potential for near-instant, low-cost, and borderless transactions, removing the need for intermediaries and reducing fees significantly. Altcoins like Ripple (XRP) and Stellar (XLM) have designed their networks to facilitate efficient cross-border payments, enabling individuals to send and receive funds across continents in seconds, rather than days.

Altcoins have also emerged as powerful tools for fostering financial inclusion, especially in regions with limited access to traditional banking services. In many parts of the world, individuals lack access to basic banking infrastructure, making saving, investing, or accessing credit challenging. The underbanked and unbanked may be able to access financial services through altcoins and blockchain technology, enabling them to engage in the global economy. Alternative cryptocurrencies (altcoins) like Litecoin (LTC) and Cardano (ADA) seek to offer solutions that enable individuals who have traditionally been shut out of the established financial system.

The rise of decentralized finance (DeFi) epitomizes the transformational potential of altcoins in shaping the future of banking and financial services. DeFi protocols built on altcoins enable individuals to lend, borrow, trade, and earn interest without relying on traditional financial intermediaries. Ethereum-based altcoins like Compound

(COMP) and Aave (AAVE) have pioneered this movement, allowing users to participate in lending and borrowing markets in a trustless and transparent manner. DeFi democratizes access to financial services and challenges the conventional banking model by creating open and permissionless financial networks.

As governments worldwide explore the development of Central Bank Digital Currencies (CBDCs), altcoins play a crucial role in shaping the discourse around digital currencies issued by central banks. CBDCs aim to merge the benefits of digital currency with the stability and backing of government entities. Altcoins contribute to this conversation by demonstrating digital currencies' technical and economic possibilities, paving the way for innovative CBDC designs and implementation strategies.

The emergence of altcoins has injected competition and innovation into the financial sector, challenging traditional financial institutions to adapt and evolve. The introduction of altcoins with unique features, such as privacy enhancements, smart contract capabilities, and cross-chain interoperability, has forced traditional banks to reconsider their approach to technology, customer experience, and service delivery. This competitive landscape benefits consumers by offering a wider range of financial goods and services that cater to diverse needs.

While altcoins hold transformative potential, their rapid development has raised regulatory questions and concerns. Different jurisdictions have varied approaches to classifying and regulating altcoins, which can impact their adoption and growth. Regulatory clarity and frameworks will significantly determine how altcoins integrate into the broader financial ecosystem and how they contribute to shaping the global financial future.

The exploration of CBDCs is deeply intertwined with the innovation and experimentation facilitated by altcoins. The emergence of altcoins has shown that digital currencies can operate on various technological platforms, each with unique characteristics. This knowledge can influence the design and implementation of CBDCs, allowing central banks to leverage the benefits of blockchain technology and programmable money.

The idea of smart contracts, which are essentially self-executing contracts with the terms of the deal explicitly put into code, was first proposed by altcoins. This innovation has far-reaching implications, enabling the automation of complex financial transactions, the creation of decentralized applications, and the emergence of entirely new business models. Integrating smart contracts into the global financial system could streamline processes, reduce counterparty risk, and enhance the efficiency of financial interactions.

The innovation, adaptability, and transformative potential of altcoins is shaping the future of the global financial system. These alternative cryptocurrencies have transcended their role as mere digital assets to become powerful agents of change across various aspects of finance. From cross-border transactions and financial inclusion to open finance and CBDC innovation, altcoins are paving the way for a more accessible, efficient, and inclusive financial ecosystem. As the world embraces the possibilities offered by altcoins, their continued development, integration, and collaboration with traditional financial systems will usher in a new era of global finance that is both innovative and inclusive.

CHAPTER VIII

Building Your Altcoin Investment Strategy

Setting investment goals and risk tolerance

Investing in altcoins, the diverse universe of alternative cryptocurrencies beyond Bitcoin, has become an increasingly popular avenue for individuals seeking to diversify their investment portfolios and take advantage of blockchain technology's possibilities. However, the altcoin market's dynamic and often volatile nature requires careful consideration and strategic planning. In this section, we delve into the essential aspects of setting investment goals and risk tolerance when engaging in altcoin investments, examining the importance of defining clear objectives, understanding risk factors, and developing a well-informed investment strategy that aligns with an individual's financial situation, aspirations, and risk appetite.

Before delving into the world of altcoin investments, it is crucial to define clear investment goals. These goals provide a roadmap for the investment journey, guiding decisions and strategies. Investment goals can vary widely, ranging from capital appreciation, income generation, funding specific financial objectives (e.g., buying a home or funding education), or simply participating in a particular sector of the altcoin market. Defining these goals helps investors remain focused and make informed decisions that are in line with their desired outcomes.

Risk tolerance is a pivotal factor in determining the level of risk an individual is willing and able to undertake in their investment ventures. Various factors, including financial situation, investment horizon, personal preferences, and emotional resilience influence it. Investors must honestly evaluate their ability to endure market fluctuations and potential losses. While altcoins can offer substantial rewards, they are also subject to higher volatility compared to more established assets like stocks or bonds.

Finding the right balance between risk and return is fundamental to successful altcoin investments. High potential returns often come with elevated risks, and individuals must weigh these factors when forming their investment strategies. The risk-return trade-off is a core principle of investment, emphasizing that higher potential returns are typically associated with higher levels of risk. Balancing this trade-off requires aligning investment goals with risk tolerance, striking a chord between the desire for growth and the capacity to manage potential losses.

The altcoin market is characterized by its unique dynamics, influenced by technological advancements, market sentiment, regulatory developments, and broader macroeconomic trends. Altcoins can experience rapid price fluctuations within short periods, driven by news events or shifts in market sentiment. Understanding these dynamics is essential for informed decision-making, as it allows investors to anticipate potential market movements and make strategic adjustments to their investment portfolio.

Diversification, the practice of spreading investments across various assets, is a crucial risk management strategy in the altcoin market. Diversifying an altcoin portfolio can mitigate the impact of poor performance by reducing the concentration of risk in a single asset. It can also provide exposure to different sectors of the altcoin market, allowing investors to capitalize on diverse growth opportunities while minimizing the potential downside of individual underperformers.

Investment goals play a central role in guiding altcoin investment decisions. For instance, if an investor's goal is capital appreciation, they may focus on altcoins with strong growth potential, even if they come with higher volatility. Conversely, an investor seeking income generation might opt for altcoins offering staking rewards or participating in decentralized finance (DeFi) platforms. Aligning investments with goals ensures that each altcoin serves a purpose within the broader portfolio strategy.

Effective altcoin investment requires thorough due diligence. Researching each altcoin's technology, team, use case, community engagement, and market potential is essential for making informed decisions. Understanding the fundamentals helps investors identify projects with solid foundations and growth potential while avoiding projects with questionable legitimacy or inadequate development efforts.

Staying informed about the rapidly evolving altcoin market is essential for successful investment management. Monitoring news, market trends, and regulatory developments can provide valuable insights into possible risks and opportunities. It's essential to be able to adapt to changing conditions so that investors can modify their plans in response to new information and changes in the market environment.

Investment decisions are heavily influenced by emotions, which frequently result in impulsive actions motivated by greed or fear. Establishing a disciplined approach to altcoin investments based on well-defined goals and risk tolerance, can help mitigate emotional decision-making. Implementing strategies such as setting stop-loss orders and sticking to a predetermined asset allocation can prevent emotional reactions to market fluctuations.

For individuals unfamiliar with the intricacies of altcoin investments, seeking professional financial advice can provide valuable guidance. Financial advisors can aid investors navigate the complexities of the altcoin market, assess risk tolerance, and tailor investment strategies to individual circumstances. Their expertise can help ensure that altcoin investments align with broader financial goals and risk tolerance.

Investing in altcoins offers an avenue for capitalizing on the revolutionary potential of blockchain technology and diversifying investment portfolios. However, success in the altcoin market requires a well-considered approach that encompasses setting clear investment goals, assessing risk tolerance, conducting diligent research, and adapting to market dynamics. By aligning investments with individual aspirations and risk appetites, and adhering to disciplined strategies, investors can navigate the altcoin landscape with a higher probability of achieving their financial objectives while managing potential risks effectively. Ultimately, the world of altcoin investments presents exciting opportunities for those who approach it with knowledge, foresight, and a commitment to prudent decision-making.

Creating a diversified altcoin portfolio

In the realm of blockchain and cryptocurrency, altcoins have emerged as a dynamic and diverse array of digital assets that extend far beyond the pioneering Bitcoin. Investors have a broad spectrum of options to diversify their portfolios and take advantage of the innovative potential of numerous blockchain projects as the altcoin market continues to develop. However, the volatility and complexity of the altcoin market require careful planning and a strategic approach to portfolio construction. In this section, we explore the principles and strategies behind creating a diversified altcoin portfolio, examining the importance of diversification, asset allocation, risk management, and the considerations contributing to a well-balanced and resilient investment strategy.

Diversification is a key aspect of investment that aims to spread risk across different assets to reduce the impact of poor performance on any single asset. In the context of altcoins, diversification involves allocating investments across various projects, technologies, and sectors within the cryptocurrency ecosystem. A diversified portfolio is designed to withstand market fluctuations and potential downturns, providing a buffer against extreme volatility characteristic of the altcoin market.

Creating a diversified altcoin portfolio begins with defining a precise asset allocation strategy. This strategy entails deciding how much of your investment capital to allocate to different altcoins, such as those with strong growth potential, stablecoins, income-generating tokens, and more. The distribution of assets within the portfolio should be aligned with an investor's risk tolerance, investment goals, and market outlook.

Diversification can extend beyond asset types to encompass different sectors within the altcoin market. Sectors might include decentralized finance (DeFi), non-fungible tokens (NFTs), privacy-focused coins, interoperability projects, and more. Each sector carries its unique risks and potential for growth, and diversifying across industries can help mitigate the impact of poor performance in a particular industry while capitalizing on opportunities in others.

Balancing risk and reward is central to creating a diversified altcoin portfolio. While high-risk projects may offer substantial returns, they also have a greater potential for loss. Conversely, lower-risk projects might provide more stability but with potentially lower returns. Balancing these elements is essential for aligning the portfolio with an individual's risk tolerance and investment goals.

Effective diversification requires thorough research into the altcoins being considered for inclusion in the portfolio. This research involves assessing factors such as the project's technology, use case, team, market potential, community engagement, and competitive landscape. A well-informed decision to include an altcoin in the portfolio is more likely to yield positive results over the long term.

The altcoin market is dynamic, and the relative performance of different assets can change over time. Portfolio rebalancing involves periodically adjusting the allocation of assets to keep the desired level of diversification. Rebalancing ensures that the portfolio's risk exposure remains aligned with an investor's risk tolerance and helps capture new growth opportunities while managing potential risks.

Altcoins are known for their price volatility, which can lead to significant fluctuations in portfolio value. Managing exposure to volatility involves considering the allocation of stablecoins or other low-volatility assets within the portfolio. These assets can act as a hedge against extreme market fluctuations and provide stability during periods of market uncertainty.

The timeframe of an investor's goals also influences portfolio diversification. A long-term investor might focus on projects with strong fundamentals and growth potential, while a short-term trader might prioritize assets with high liquidity and frequent price movements. Understanding one's investment horizon helps guide the choice of altcoins and their allocation within the portfolio.

Maintaining a diversified altcoin portfolio requires ongoing monitoring and staying informed about market trends, news, and developments. Staying up-to-date allows investors to make informed decisions about when to adjust allocations, take advantage of new opportunities, or reallocate assets based on changing market dynamics.

Creating a diversified altcoin portfolio is a strategic endeavor that combines art and science. It involves crafting a blend of assets that align with an investor's financial objectives and risk tolerance and reflect an understanding of the unique characteristics of the altcoin market. A well-constructed diversified portfolio seeks to achieve resilience in the face of uncertainty, capturing growth opportunities while mitigating potential losses. By adhering to the principles of diversification, asset allocation, and ongoing monitoring, investors can navigate the complex altcoin landscape with greater confidence, poised to capitalize on the transformative possibility of blockchain technology while minimizing risks. Ultimately, building a diversified altcoin portfolio requires a blend of knowledge, foresight, and the ability to adapt to the ever-evolving dynamics of the cryptocurrency ecosystem.

Portfolio management and tracking tools

Investing in altcoins, the diverse and dynamic world of alternative cryptocurrencies, presents exciting opportunities and unique challenges. As the altcoin market evolves, investors face the task of managing a portfolio that spans various assets, sectors, and strategies. To navigate this complex landscape successfully, investors rely on portfolio management and tracking tools that offer insights, organization, risk assessment, and the ability to make informed decisions. In this section, we delve into the essential role of portfolio management and tracking tools for investing in altcoins, exploring their benefits, features, and how they empower investors to optimize their portfolios and navigate the fast-paced and ever-changing altcoin market effectively.

As the altcoin market expands, managing a portfolio of diverse digital assets becomes increasingly complex. Altcoins vary in terms of technology, use case, risk profile, and market dynamics. Effective portfolio management is essential for aligning investment strategies with financial goals, minimizing risks, capturing growth opportunities, and ensuring that an investor's portfolio evolves in line with the dynamic altcoin ecosystem.

Portfolio tracking tools give investors real-time insights into their altcoin holdings, overall portfolio performance, and market trends. These tools aggregate data from multiple exchanges and sources, enabling investors to monitor their investments' value, price movements, trading volumes, and historical performance. This information empowers investors to make educated decisions, whether it involves reallocating assets, adjusting risk exposure, or taking advantage of market trends.

Diversification and asset allocation are critical principles in altcoin investment. Portfolio management tools assist investors in maintaining a well-balanced portfolio by displaying the allocation of assets across different altcoins, sectors, and risk profiles. These tools visually represent an investor's exposure, helping them assess whether their portfolio aligns with their diversification goals and risk tolerance.

Investing in altcoins involves inherent risks due to market volatility and the evolving nature of blockchain projects. Portfolio management tools offer risk assessment features that allow investors to evaluate the overall risk profile of their holdings. They may provide metrics such as the portfolio's volatility, value at risk (VaR), and other risk indicators. This information helps investors understand the potential downside and make knowledgeable decisions about risk management strategies.

Performance tracking tools provide a holistic view of an investor's altcoin portfolio performance over different timeframes. They allow investors to compare their portfolio's performance against various benchmarks, such as market indices or other altcoin portfolios. This feature helps investors gauge whether their investments are outperforming or underperforming relative to market trends and industry standards.

In the fast-paced altcoin market, staying informed is crucial. Portfolio tracking tools often offer real-time alerts and notifications for price movements, news, and market events related to an investor's holdings. These alerts help investors respond swiftly to changing market conditions, enabling them to make timely decisions about portfolio adjustments.

For investors navigating the complexities of cryptocurrency taxation, some portfolio management tools offer features that facilitate tax reporting and compliance. These tools track trades, purchases, sales, and other transactions, generating reports that simplify the process of calculating capital gains and losses for tax purposes.

Managing multiple altcoin investments across various exchanges can be challenging. Portfolio tracking tools simplify record-keeping by automatically aggregating transaction data from different platforms. This streamlines the process of reconciling trades, monitoring balances, and ensuring accurate and up-to-date records of holdings.

Rebalancing a portfolio involves periodically adjusting the allocation of assets to maintain desired risk exposure and target asset allocations. Some portfolio management tools offer automation features that facilitate this process. Investors can set target allocations, and the tool will automatically trigger rebalancing actions when allocations deviate from the desired levels.

Many portfolio tracking tools integrate with exchange APIs, allowing investors to link their exchange accounts directly to the tool. This integration enables real-time data synchronization, reducing the need for manual data entry and offering accurate and up-to-date portfolio information.

Different investors have unique preferences and strategies. Portfolio management tools often provide customization options that allow investors to tailor the tool's features to their specific needs. This includes setting custom watchlists, creating custom alerts, and categorizing holdings based on personal criteria.

In the rapidly evolving altcoin market, where innovation and disruption are constants, effective portfolio management, and tracking tools are indispensable assets for investors seeking success. These tools offer insights, organization, risk assessment, and the ability to make knowldegeable decisions based on real-time data and analysis. Whether it's assessing risk, tracking performance, rebalancing allocations, or simplifying tax reporting, portfolio management tools provide the foundation for a well-informed and strategic approach to altcoin investments. By harnessing the power of technology to navigate the complexities of the altcoin ecosystem, investors are empowered to optimize their portfolios, capture growth opportunities, and navigate the challenges of this dynamic and transformative landscape with precision and confidence.

Adapting strategies based on market trends

Investing in the world of altcoins, the diverse and dynamic universe of alternative cryptocurrencies, requires a multifaceted approach that responds to the ever-evolving nature of the market. As blockchain technology advances and new projects emerge, market trends in the altcoin space can shift rapidly, presenting both opportunities and challenges for investors. Adapting investment strategies based on these trends is crucial to capitalize on growth prospects and manage risks effectively. In this section, we delve into the significance of adapting strategies based on market trends when investing in altcoins, exploring the benefits of staying informed, recognizing key trends, and adjusting investment approaches to navigate the complexities of this fast-paced and transformative landscape.

The altcoin market is marked by its fluidity, with trends that can change rapidly due to technological advancements, regulatory developments, market sentiment, and macroeconomic shifts. Staying attuned to these trends is essential for investors seeking to make informed decisions and harness opportunities as they arise.

Adapting strategies based on market trends begins with thorough research and analysis. Investors must continuously learn about the altcoin market, understand the technology behind different projects, evaluate their use cases, assess market sentiment, and track the progress of ongoing developments. Robust research forms the foundation for identifying emerging trends and strategically adjusting investment portfolios.

Like other financial markets, Altcoin markets experience cycles of bull and bear phases. A bull market is distinguished by rising prices and positive sentiment, while declining prices and pessimism mark a bear market. Adapting strategies during these phases is crucial. In a bull market, investors focus on capitalizing on growth opportunities, while in a bear market, they prioritize risk management and preservation of capital.

Blockchain technology evolves rapidly, leading to continuous innovation in the altcoin space. Projects that introduce groundbreaking features, scalability improvements, privacy enhancements, or interoperability solutions can drive market trends. Investors who stay informed about these technological advancements can adapt their strategies to include projects that harness new capabilities and potentially disrupt existing industries.

Regulatory changes can significantly impact the altcoin market. Investors must be vigilant about legal developments in different jurisdictions, as regulations can influence market sentiment and project viability. Adapting strategies to account for regulatory shifts helps investors manage risks associated with changing compliance requirements.

The rise of decentralized finance (DeFi) and non-fungible tokens (NFTs) has reshaped the altcoin landscape. Adapting strategies to incorporate exposure to these sectors can allow investors to capitalize on the growth potential of innovative financial products, lending platforms, liquidity pools, and unique digital assets.

Market sentiment plays a significant role in altcoin price movements. Positive news can lead to price rallies, while negative news can trigger sell-offs. Adapting strategies involves gauging market sentiment through social media, news platforms, and community engagement to anticipate potential shifts and make timely adjustments.

Technical analysis involves studying price charts, patterns, and indicators to forecast potential price movements. Adapting strategies based on technical analysis can help investors identify entry and exit points, manage risk, and make decisions aligned with the market's short-term trends.

Striking a balance between long-term fundamentals and short-term trends is essential. While focusing on the long-term potential of altcoin projects is crucial, adapting strategies to capture short-term trends can lead to opportunities for profit-taking and risk management.

As market trends change, portfolio rebalancing and reallocation become essential. Adapting strategies involves adjusting asset allocations to reflect shifting market dynamics and ensuring that the portfolio remains aligned with an investor's goals and risk tolerance.

Studying historical market trends can provide valuable insights into how the altcoin market has responded to various events and developments in the past. Adapting strategies based on lessons from history can help investors anticipate potential trends and respond effectively to similar situations in the future.

Adapting strategies based on market trends is a hallmark of successful altcoin investing. The altcoin landscape is marked by its fluidity, with technological innovations, regulatory changes, and market sentiment driving trend shifts. Staying informed, conducting thorough research, embracing new technologies, and staying agile in response to evolving market dynamics are all key components of effective strategy adaptation. By aligning investment decisions with emerging trends, investors can position themselves to harness growth opportunities, manage risks, and navigate the altcoin arena with confidence and precision. As the altcoin market continues to evolve, those who adeptly adapt their strategies will be better equipped to thrive in this dynamic and transformative ecosystem.

CONCLUSION

Recap of key insights covered in the book

The journey through the book "Crypto Horizons: Beyond Bitcoin - Unraveling the Potential of Altcoins and New Crypto Projects" has been a comprehensive exploration of the multifaceted world of alternative cryptocurrencies, offering readers insights into the diverse landscape of altcoins, their historical context, technological innovations, market dynamics, investment strategies, and the broader impact on the global financial system. As we recap the key insights covered throughout the book, it becomes evident that altcoins represent a significant departure from Bitcoin and a gateway to innovation, investment opportunities, and transformative change in the realm of blockchain technology and finance.

Understanding Altcoins and Their Differentiation from Bitcoin:
The book commenced by demystifying altcoins and establishing their distinction from Bitcoin. While Bitcoin paved the way for cryptocurrencies, altcoins represent a broader spectrum of digital assets with diverse use cases, technologies, and goals. This differentiation lays the groundwork for exploring the unique attributes and opportunities that altcoins bring to the table.

Historical Context: The Evolution of Altcoins and Their Purpose:
Taking a historical perspective, the book delved into the evolution of altcoins, tracing their origins to the early days

of cryptocurrency. Altcoins emerged as a response to Bitcoin's limitations, aiming to address specific shortcomings, introduce new features, and cater to distinct market niches. This historical context illuminated the purpose of altcoins as instruments of innovation, experimentation, and specialization.

Categories of Altcoins: Forks, Tokens, and Independent Blockchains:

The book provided a comprehensive breakdown of altcoin categories, exploring forks, tokens, and independent blockchains. Forks, including hard and soft forks, contribute to blockchain evolution, while tokens leverage existing blockchains for various functions, such as utility, security, or asset representation. Independent blockchains enable altcoins to develop unique ecosystems and use cases, fostering diversity in the cryptocurrency landscape.

The Role of Altcoins in the Broader Crypto Ecosystem:

Altcoins emerged as more than mere counterparts to Bitcoin; they play distinct roles in the broader crypto ecosystem. Some altcoins, such as stablecoins, serve as stable value stores, facilitating transactions and trading. Others empower decentralized finance (DeFi) platforms, enhance privacy, enable cross-chain interoperability, or explore novel consensus mechanisms, expanding the frontiers of blockchain application.

Factors Influencing the Value and Potential of Altcoins:

The book highlighted critical factors that influence the value and potential of altcoins. These factors encompass technological innovation, market demand, adoption trends, regulatory developments, and macroeconomic influences. Understanding these drivers is essential for investors seeking to make informed decisions and capitalize on altcoin growth prospects.

Technology and Innovation: Exploring Unique Features of Different Altcoins:
Technology emerged as a defining aspect of altcoins, shaping their use cases and capabilities. The book examined the unique features of various altcoins, including smart contracts, privacy-enhancing protocols, scalability solutions, and consensus mechanisms. These technological innovations underline the diversity and transformative potential of altcoins.

Market Demand and Real-World Applications of Altcoins:
Real-world applications constitute a significant driving force behind the altcoin market. From facilitating cross-border remittances to enabling decentralized applications and powering supply chain solutions, altcoins are being integrated into various industries. The book explored how altcoins contribute to innovation across sectors and drive blockchain technology adoption.

Team and Development Community: Assessing Credibility and Expertise:

Behind every successful altcoin project lies a dedicated team and community of developers. The book emphasized the importance of assessing these teams' credibility, expertise, and dedication. The likelihood of a project's long-term success is increased by a strong team with a track record of effective development and community engagement.

Volatility and Market Risks Associated with Altcoins:

The book illuminated the reality of volatility and market risks inherent in the altcoin space. While altcoins offer the potential for substantial returns, they also carry a higher degree of price fluctuation compared to traditional assets. Recognizing this volatility and employing risk management strategies are essential for investors navigating the altcoin market.

Regulatory Challenges and Legal Considerations with Altcoins:

The regulatory landscape emerged as a significant consideration for altcoin investors. The book examined the challenges posed by varying regulatory frameworks worldwide and highlighted the importance of understanding compliance requirements and seeking legal counsel to ensure responsible and compliant participation in the altcoin ecosystem.

Scams and Fraudulent Projects with Altcoins: How to Identify and Avoid Them:

The book provided insights into the risks of scams and fraudulent projects within the altcoin space. It equipped readers with tools to identify red flags, perform due diligence, and distinguish genuine projects from fraud. Vigilance, research, and skepticism emerged as key factors in avoiding potential pitfalls.

Portfolio Management and Tracking Tools for Investing in Altcoins:

Effective portfolio management and tracking tools were considered invaluable assets for altcoin investors. These tools offer insights, organization, risk assessment, and the ability to make knowledgeable judgements based on real-time data and analysis. They enable investors to optimize portfolios, navigate market trends, and adapt strategies to changing dynamics.

Adapting Strategies Based on Market Trends for Investing in Altcoins:

The book emphasized the importance of agility in response to market trends. Altcoin markets are dynamic, and strategies must adapt to technological advancements, regulatory shifts, and changing market sentiment. Staying informed, conducting thorough research, and making timely adjustments are key to capitalizing on growth prospects and managing risks.

Shaping the Future of the Global Financial System with Altcoins:

The book concluded by examining how altcoins are shaping the future of the global financial system. Altcoins are at the forefront of disrupting traditional finance, enabling financial inclusion, reducing intermediaries, and revolutionizing cross-border transactions. Their impact on payments, banking, and decentralized finance (DeFi) is reshaping the financial landscape.

In conclusion, the book journey through "Crypto Horizons: Beyond Bitcoin - Unraveling the Potential of Altcoins and New Crypto Projects" has illuminated the vast and transformative potential of altcoins. From their historical evolution to technological innovations, market dynamics, investment strategies, and their role in shaping the future, altcoins stand as a testament to the power of blockchain technology. As investors and enthusiasts continue to explore this dynamic realm, the insights shared in this book provide a foundation for making informed decisions, navigating challenges, and embracing the opportunities in the altcoin universe.

Encouraging responsible and informed altcoin investing

Investing in altcoins, the diverse array of alternative cryptocurrencies, presents an exciting journey into innovation, disruption, and financial potential. However, the altcoin market is also marked by complexity, volatility, and risks that demand a responsible and informed approach. In this section, we delve into the imperative of responsible and knowledgeable altcoin investing, exploring the importance of education, risk management, due diligence, ethical considerations, and the role of regulatory compliance. By adopting a cautious yet proactive mindset, investors can confidently navigate the altcoin landscape, mitigate risks, and contribute to the sustainable growth of the broader cryptocurrency ecosystem.

The journey to responsible and informed altcoin investing begins with education. Understanding the fundamentals of blockchain technology, the unique features of different altcoins, market dynamics, and investment strategies is crucial. Education equips investors with the tools to make informed decisions, identify potential red flags, and discern genuine projects from fraud.

Altcoins offer the potential for substantial returns, but they also carry a higher risk than traditional investments. Responsible investing involves balancing the allure of high rewards with a realistic assessment of potential losses. Diversification, asset allocation, and setting risk tolerance limits help investors manage risk exposure effectively.

Due diligence is an integral component of responsible investing in altcoins. Investigating a project's technology, use case, team, market potential, and community engagement helps mitigate the risk of investing in fraudulent or poorly executed projects. Thorough research provides the information needed to make well-founded investment decisions.

Ethics play a role in responsible investing, and the altcoin ecosystem is no exception. Investors have the power to support projects that align with ethical values and contribute positively to society. Projects prioritizing environmental sustainability, social impact, and ethical use cases resonate with responsible investors who seek financial gains and positive change.

Navigating the complex regulatory landscape is a cornerstone of responsible altcoin investing. Regulatory requirements vary by jurisdiction and impact market sentiment, project viability, and investor protection. Staying informed about local laws and seeking legal counsel ensures compliance and safeguards investments from potential legal risks.

Market manipulation is a concern in the altcoin space, with activities like pump-and-dump schemes and insider trading posing risks to investors. Responsible investing involves being cautious of exaggerated claims, sudden price spikes, and unverified information that can indicate potential manipulation. Sound judgment and skepticism are essential when evaluating market trends.

Responsible investing extends beyond short-term gains, focusing on long-term value creation and sustainability. Projects with solid technical foundations, real-world applications, and fundamentals are more likely to withstand market swings and have long-term growth potential. Investors with a long-term vision contribute to the overall maturation of the altcoin ecosystem.

Every investment involves a risk-reward trade-off. Responsible investors carefully assess this balance by considering their financial goals, risk tolerance, and the potential impact of losses on their overall portfolio. Being mindful of this assessment helps investors make prudent decisions aligned with their individual circumstances.

Skepticism and critical thinking are assets in the altcoin landscape. Responsible investors question claims, scrutinize projects, and evaluate the credibility of information sources. By exercising critical thinking, investors can avoid falling victim to misleading narratives or fraudulent schemes.

Staying informed about market trends, technological advancements, regulatory updates, and industry developments is an ongoing commitment. Responsible investors cultivate a habit of continuous learning, allowing them to adapt to changing circumstances, anticipate trends, and make well-informed decisions.

Engaging with the altcoin community fosters knowledge sharing, collaboration, and collective growth. Responsible investors participate in discussions, share insights, and contribute to the ecosystem's development. By actively engaging, investors expand their understanding and contribute to the responsible growth of the altcoin space.

In conclusion, encouraging responsible and informed altcoin investing is paramount to harnessing the transformative potential of cryptocurrencies. Education, risk management, due diligence, ethical considerations, regulatory compliance, and critical thinking are pillars of responsible investing. By adhering to these principles, investors protect their interests and contribute to the altcoin ecosystem's maturation and sustainability. As the cryptocurrency landscape evolves, responsible and informed investors stand as guardians of progress, ensuring that the promise of blockchain technology is realized in a responsible, ethical, and beneficial manner for individuals and society at large.

The evolving landscape of cryptocurrencies and the role of altcoins

The world of cryptocurrencies has undergone a remarkable evolution since the inception of Bitcoin in 2009. What began as an experimental digital currency has become a global phenomenon reshaping finance, technology, and even social dynamics. Central to this evolution is the emergence of altcoins, a term encompassing a diverse array of alternative cryptocurrencies beyond Bitcoin. In this section, we explore the ever-evolving landscape of cryptocurrencies and the pivotal role that altcoins play within it. From technological advancements to market trends, regulatory shifts, and the broader impact on the global financial system, this exploration sheds light on the transformative journey of cryptocurrencies and the diverse opportunities offered by altcoins.

The journey into the evolving cryptocurrency landscape begins with Bitcoin, the pioneer that introduced the concept of a decentralized digital currency. Bitcoin's decentralized nature, powered by blockchain technology, ignited a paradigm shift in the financial sector. Its emergence as a store of value and medium of exchange sparked interest in the possibilities of digital assets, leading to the birth of altcoins.

Altcoins represent a departure from the one-size-fits-all approach of Bitcoin. These alternative cryptocurrencies leverage blockchain technology to address specific shortcomings, introduce novel features, and cater to diverse use cases. Ethereum, for instance, introduced smart contracts and enabled the creation of decentralized applications (DApps), while Litecoin focused on enhancing transaction speed. The evolution of altcoins heralded a new era of innovation and experimentation in the cryptocurrency space.

Technological innovations have been instrumental in shaping the diverse landscape of altcoins. Projects like Ripple (XRP) aimed to revolutionize cross-border payments, IOTA introduced the concept of the Internet of Things (IoT) transactions, and Monero (XMR) prioritized privacy enhancements. Each altcoin contributes unique technological features that cater to specific industries and use cases.

The evolving landscape of altcoins is closely intertwined with market trends and adoption. Altcoins experience cycles of innovation and consolidation, with projects rising and falling based on market demand, technological advancements, and investor sentiment. The rise of decentralized finance (DeFi) and non-fungible tokens (NFTs) further underscores the dynamic nature of altcoin adoption and usage.

The evolution of the altcoin market is significantly influenced by the regulatory environment. Altcoin projects must traverse a difficult legal environment as governments and regulatory organizations struggle with the classification, taxation, and oversight of cryptocurrencies. Regulatory clarity impacts market sentiment, project viability, and investor confidence, underscoring the need for responsible engagement and compliance.

Altcoins are more than mere alternatives to Bitcoin; they serve as catalysts for innovation. Beyond their financial applications, altcoins drive technological advancements, encourage creative solutions, and foster collaboration among developers and industries. Projects like Cardano (ADA) prioritize research-driven development, contributing to the broader blockchain ecosystem's growth.

Decentralization is a core principle of cryptocurrencies, and altcoins are pivotal in advancing this ethos. The diverse altcoin ecosystem promotes competition, encourages experimentation, and prevents a single project from monopolizing the space. This decentralized landscape empowers users, enhances security, and mitigates systemic risks.

The emergence of decentralized finance (DeFi) has further elevated the role of altcoins. DeFi platforms harness altcoins to create innovative financial products, from lending and borrowing protocols to automated market makers. This convergence of technology, finance, and altcoins is reshaping traditional financial systems and democratizing access to financial services.

Stablecoins, a subset of altcoins, bridge the gap between traditional and cryptocurrency finance. Pegged to stable assets like fiat currencies or commodities, stablecoins offer price stability and serve as on-ramps for new users entering the cryptocurrency ecosystem. They facilitate seamless transitions between the traditional and digital financial worlds.

The global impact of altcoins extends beyond financial markets. Altcoins contribute to financial inclusion by providing access to banking services for the unbanked. They enable cross-border remittances with reduced fees and offer secure and transparent supply chain solutions. Altcoins also empower individuals in regions with unstable economies, offering an alternative to traditional financial systems.

The evolution of cryptocurrencies and the role of altcoins reflect a dynamic and transformative future. From the early days of Bitcoin to the proliferation of diverse altcoin projects, the landscape has evolved rapidly. Technological innovation, market trends, regulatory changes, and the drive for decentralized finance have combined to reshape the global financial system. As the journey continues, the role of altcoins remains central to unlocking the potential of blockchain technology and revolutionizing how we envision, transact, and interact with financial systems worldwide.

Final thoughts on the future potential of altcoins

As we stand at the intersection of technology, finance, and innovation, the future potential of altcoins shines brightly, illuminating a path toward a transformed global landscape. The journey through the realm of cryptocurrencies has been nothing short of extraordinary, with altcoins emerging as a driving force behind the evolution of this digital revolution. In this section, we delve into the final thoughts on the future potential of altcoins, exploring the factors contributing to their enduring significance, the challenges they face, and their role in shaping a new era of decentralized possibilities.

At the heart of the future potential of altcoins lies the power of innovation. These alternative cryptocurrencies have shattered the limitations of traditional finance, ushering in a new era of creative solutions and technological advancements. With each altcoin project designed to address unique challenges and embrace specific use cases, innovation becomes the catalyst that propels the entire ecosystem forward.

The future potential of altcoins extends beyond their individual achievements; it is rooted in the diversity they bring to the broader cryptocurrency landscape. Altcoins create a flourishing ecosystem marked by competition, collaboration, and specialization. This diverse tapestry allows for the exploration of novel ideas, the refinement of existing technologies, and the establishment of a truly inclusive digital financial realm.

Altcoins are not confined to the realm of technology and finance; they are poised to transform traditional industries. From supply chain management to healthcare, altcoins offer the potential to promote security, transparency, and efficiency across sectors. Their role as facilitators of decentralized applications holds the promise of a more equitable and accountable global economy.

One of the most profound aspects of the future potential of altcoins is their role in democratizing finance. These cryptocurrencies break down barriers, granting access to financial services to individuals who have been historically excluded. Through decentralized lending, borrowing, and remittance platforms, altcoins empower individuals around the world to participate in the global economy.

The future potential of altcoins also reshapes investment paradigms. As traditional assets undergo shifts and uncertainties, altcoins offer a unique opportunity for diversification and exposure to high-growth sectors. While risks remain, the potential for substantial returns has attracted investors seeking novel avenues for wealth creation.

However, the road to realizing the future potential of altcoins is not without its challenges. Regulatory hurdles cast a shadow over the landscape, as governments grapple with the classification and oversight of cryptocurrencies. Striking a balance between innovation and compliance is essential to ensure a stable and supportive regulatory environment that fosters responsible growth.

The evolving nature of altcoins introduces technological complexity that demands continuous learning and adaptation. As projects incorporate intricate features, consensus mechanisms, and interoperability solutions, investors and users alike must navigate this complexity to harness the potential of altcoins fully.

The inherent volatility of the altcoin market remains a critical consideration. While potential gains are enticing, they come hand in hand with the risk of significant losses. Responsible risk management, thorough research, and strategic portfolio diversification are vital to navigate this volatility effectively.

The future potential of altcoins is not solely about individual projects; it thrives on collaboration. Altcoins leverage the collective knowledge and expertise of developers, communities, and investors to drive progress. Collaborative efforts enhance the ecosystem's robustness, fostering an environment where innovation can flourish.

Ultimately, the future potential of altcoins aligns with the broader goal of shaping a decentralized future. This future transcends financial systems; it envisions a world where power is distributed, trust is inherent, and individuals have sovereignty over their digital identities and assets. With their diverse applications and innovations, Altcoins are at the forefront of this transformative journey.

In conclusion, the future potential of altcoins represents a new dawn of possibilities that stretches far beyond the confines of traditional financial systems. These alternative cryptocurrencies are the driving force behind innovation, inclusion, and decentralization. They promise to transform industries, democratize finance, and reshape the way we perceive and interact with value. While challenges persist, the commitment of visionaries, developers, investors, and enthusiasts propels the altcoin ecosystem forward. As we navigate this uncharted territory, it is clear that the future potential of altcoins lies not only in their financial gains but in the profound impact they stand to make on the world—a world marked by innovation, empowerment, and the dawn of a decentralized future.

Thank you for buying and reading/ listening to our book. If you found this book useful/ helpful please take a few minutes and leave a review on the platform where you purchased our book. Your feedback matters greatly to us.